W9-BPJ-882

Training Your Beagle

Kristine Kraeuter

Kristine Kraeuter '01

BARRON'S

Cover Credits

Norvia Behling: inside front cover, inside back cover, back cover; Isabelle Francais: front cover.

Photo Credits

Norvia Behling: page viii; Mandy Bobbitt: pages 8, 103 (bottom); Joel Brandt: page 91; Lori Bulmer: pages 106, 112; Lisa Campbell: pages 102, 117; Jeff Chukalochak: pages 10, 81 (right); Bev Cigler and Kent Crawford: page 97; Karen Dale: pages 113, 124, 126 (top left, top right, and bottom), 127, 128 (left and right); William Eickmaer: page 125; Kristine Kraeuter: pages 13, 19, 20, 23, 24, 26, 28, 29, 33, 35, 42, 44 (left and right), 46, 47, 55, 56, 59, 61, 67 (left and right), 72, 76, 84, 85, 86, 93, 100, 103 (top), 108, 111 (top and bottom); 116, 118, 120, 121, 129, 132, 135, 138, 139,144; Marie Morris: page 90 (left and right); Claudia Pelzmann: pages 2, 3, 4, 5, 11, 14, 15, 16, 22, 30, 38, 50, 52, 57, 63, 81 (left), 82, 94, 98, 115, 122, 131; Jon Woodring: page 136.

All inquiries should be addressed to:
Barron's Educational Series, Inc.
250 Wireless Boulevard
Hauppauge, NY 11788
http://www.barronseduc.com

International Standard Book No. 0-7641-1648-7
Library of Congress Catalog Card No. 00-049810

Library of Congress Cataloging-in-Publication Data
Kraeuter, Kristine.
    Training your beagle / Kristine Kraeuter.
      p. cm.
    Includes bibliographical references (p.).
    ISBN 0-7641-1648-7
      1. Beagle (Dog breed)—Training. I. Title.

SF429.B3 K73 2001
636.753'735—dc21   00-049810

Printed in Hong Kong
9 8 7 6 5 4 3 2 1

About the Author

Kristine Kraeuter is a breeder/trainer/handler of Beagles with a disposition toward promoting versatility in the breed. She has written extensively on canine topics, ranging from conformation to field work to responsible breeding practices, for numerous publications. Kraeuter is an active member of the National Beagle Club of America and an honorary whipper-in for the Holly Hill Pack. *Training Your Beagle* is her first book project for Barron's.

Acknowledgments

This book is dedicated to the memory of my dear friend and mentor, the late Robert Felty. Bob was a tremendously generous individual, who graciously shared with us his 50-plus years of experience and knowledge regarding Beagles and scenthounds. His Felty's Beagles are to be found within the pedigrees of many of the finest conformation Beagles throughout the world today.

    I wish to extend my sincerest thanks to all of the Beagle owners who contributed to this work in so many different ways—through encouragement and suggestions, written contributions, and sharing photographs of wonderful examples of the Beagle breed. Too numerous to name individually here, many are acknowledged throughout this book or in the photo credits. Special thanks go to my family, particularly Jack and Matthew, for being patient with me while I was working on this manuscript. Thanks also to Wanda Borsa for introducing me to organized pack Beagling and the NBC...and especially to our foundation Beagle at Brushyrun, CH. Brierwood's Blaze Starr.

Important Note

This book tells the reader how to train a Beagle. The author and the publisher consider it important to point out that the advice given in the book is meant primarily for normally developed puppies from a good breeder—that is, dogs of excellent physical health and good character.

    Anyone who adopts a fully grown dog should be aware that the animal has already formed its basic impressions of human beings. There are dogs that as a result of bad experiences with humans behave in an unnatural manner or may even bite. Only people that have experience with dogs should take in such an animal.

    Even well-behaved and carefully supervised dogs sometimes do damage to someone else's property or cause accidents. It is, therefore, in the owner's interest to be adequately insured against such eventualities, and we strongly urge all dog owners to purchase a liability policy that covers their dog.

Contents

1 Introduction

Why Do You Need to Train?

Training your Beagle to behave appropriately is a fundamental part of responsible dog ownership. A well-behaved, obedient canine is a pleasure to live with. Through proper training, your Beagle will learn what is expected of him, understand how best to please his human companions, and will become a more welcome and appreciated member of the family. As a good neighbor and responsible member of the community, you should want your hound to exhibit appropriate manners and behavior, be completely reliable around children, and never pose a threat to others. This all can be accomplished through a commitment to provide consistent, basic manners training.

An untrained Beagle, in contrast, can quickly become a nuisance. He soils your house, chews anything within reach, and in general can make life quite miserable for everyone around him. His inappropriate barking and other bad manners may bring disapproval from the neighbors, and each incidence contributes to the antidog sentiment that impacts all of us as dog owners. Far too many families go month after month, year after year, unnecessarily tolerating the misbehaviors of a disobedient dog.

Benefits of Training

Training involves all aspects of how a dog interacts with his human family members, and with the community at large. The benefits of owning a well-mannered, obedience-trained hound are many.

■ Training serves to strengthen the bond between the Beagle and his owner while subtly yet effectively establishing your position as *pack leader*. It easily

---

Note: Beagles are especially intelligent, perceptive little hounds, generally eager to please their masters. But they are not born into the world programmed with the knowledge of what their human family will consider appropriate and inappropriate behavior. This is why it is important for you to provide proper training and guidance in order to help your Beagle become the polite companion you hope for.

A group of polite canine companions is shown here.

establishes a sense of social hierarchy. These little hounds are especially pack oriented, and it is important that they understand their place in the pack and respect your position as the *alpha* pack member.

■ A well-trained dog is a happier dog. Because he knows the rules of appropriate behavior, an obedient Beagle is more reliable and thus requires fewer restrictions. His good manners often earn him more attention and interaction from family members, houseguests, and the general public.

■ Training opens up the lines of communication between you and your Beagle, builds understanding, and fosters a mutual respect. Providing gentle guidance and a consistent set of rules to live by helps to build your hound's confidence and promotes a sense of security.

■ Obedience training can save your dog's life. By teaching him to respond to basic commands, you can exercise immediate control over your Beagle's actions in an emergency situation. Training your hound to respond to commands such as *"Come," "Sit," and "Leave It!"* can help prevent tragedy and are useful in a multitude of potentially dangerous situations. An educated Beagle understands his boundaries, suffers less boredom, and is therefore less likely to engage in dangerous mischief. He should also be comfortable with your handling of any part of his body, willingly allowing you to check for injuries or illness and to administer medications.

■ Training should be satisfying and rewarding for both you and your Beagle. Basic manners training will enrich your relationship and lay the foundation for possible participation in more advanced canine activities such as competitive Obedience, Agility, field trials, or conformation shows.

Natural Canine Behavior

The majority of perceived behavioral problems in dogs are the result of perfectly normal canine conduct that has been misdirected or occurs at an inappropriate time or location. Without proper guidance and supervision, your Beagle will likely behave according to his natural animal instincts and in keeping with the hundreds of years of selective breeding that resulted in this tenacious little hunting hound. Thus, manners training is primarily aimed at modifying and redirecting your Beagle's natural behaviors toward outlets that are more acceptable in a domestic situation.

Wild Canines and Pack Instinct

The inherent behaviors and instincts possessed by the wild ancestors of our modern-day domesticated dog were focused primarily on simple survival. Through natural selection canines developed that possessed those physical and mental attributes best suited for perpetuation of the species. These wild dogs

found it advantageous to live in groups known as *packs*. Cooperation in chasing down and killing their prey helped to ensure an adequate food supply, and pack members likely also found a sense of security and safety in numbers.

Because participation within the group afforded dogs numerous benefits, many of their instinctive behaviors centered around pack interactions and maintaining a social hierarchy. Our modern Beagles continue to act a great deal according to pack instincts. This is due in part to their selective development as scenthounds that have been, throughout much of their history, typically housed and used for hunting as a pack. To preserve order, individual hounds must learn their respective positions within the pack, and then maintain those positions through behavioral interactions. While some dogs will occasionally challenge their dominants in an attempt

Training fosters mutual respect.

3

to improve their ranking within the pack hierarchy, harmony is generally maintained through physical posturing and minor altercations. Serious conflicts that might result in grave injury rarely occur.

Inherited Behavior Patterns

As a member of the canine family, your Beagle shares many of these same ingrained instincts and needs. An instinct is defined as an inborn, precise form of behavior. There is no knowledge behind instinct; instinctual behaviors originate from within and are hereditary, not learned.

Specific instincts that were favorable for survival have become fixed in the genetic material of our dogs through natural selection. Other behavior patterns

Following his nose comes naturally.

have been enhanced or altered by humans through selective breeding. Because of this heredity, breeds of dogs have been developed that do not need to be taught to perform the fundamental tasks for which they were selectively bred. No one teaches a well-bred Beagle to use his nose to follow the scent of a rabbit, or to bay while in hot pursuit; it is a natural, inherited behavior that he cannot help but act on.

A basic understanding of instinctual behaviors can aid us in our approach to training the Beagle. In addition to *packing*, the following actions helped the wild ancestors of our modern dogs to survive.

■ Digging holes provided protection. A hole in the ground might serve as a place to escape the wind and weather in order to stay warm, or as a cool spot during hot weather. A large hole, or den, provided a safe place to whelp and raise pups.

■ Barking is used as a means of warning pack members of intruders or potential danger. Additionally, it serves as a signal to alert others of an individual's location, such as when a Beagle gives voice upon finding an interesting scent, calling in his packmates to join in the hunt. Dogs also may learn to use vocalizations as a form of communication in order to elicit a desired response.

■ Scent marking through urination and other means is used by canines to delineate their territory and declare ownership. Marking is also used as a method of leaving a "calling card," or in the case of a female in heat, as advertisement that she is ready for mating.

Beagles are very pack oriented.

While many of the behaviors of dogs are instinctual, others are the result of experience and education. It might be said that instinct forms the foundation, while learning helps to perfect the inherited behavior patterns and influences the direction those patterns might take.

Shaping Your Ideal Beagle Companion

Instinctual behaviors come quite naturally to our Beagles, yet many are simply unacceptable if the hound is to be a welcome part of our home and family. No one wants to live with a dog that is constantly threatening and attempting to dominate the human members of his *pack*. We don't want our little hounds urinating throughout the household, digging holes in the sofa, or barking excessively. The solution? We are not going to allow our Beagles to act on their own, simply following their instincts and learning by trial and error. Through training we can shape and channel the dog's behavior toward more acceptable outlets, making him a pleasant, well-mannered family companion.

As we prepare to embark into a positive training program, it is important to remember that every dog is different. Your approach to training will be governed a great deal by the dog you have on the other end of the leash. Understanding the function for which the Beagle has been selectively bred will help you to find an appropriate way in which to encourage him to express his natural talents. It will also allow you to be aware of how and when those same inherited instincts might present a challenge.

History of the Beagle

Beagle Breed Origin

Before we embark on a discussion on training your Beagle companion, it is worthwhile to review this merry little hound's history and the original purpose for which he was bred. Understanding where the Beagle came from, and the hundreds of years of selective breeding that have gone into developing this industrious scenthound will help us to better comprehend the typical breed temperament and how best to approach his training.

The earliest surviving manuscript to document the use of dogs in connection with hunting other animals, the *Onomasticon* (a Greek dictionary compiled by Iulius Pollux during the second century A.D.) records the use of canines for hunting around 1300 B.C. Geologists tend to believe that it may have been closer to 5000 B.C. when humans first tamed and employed the domestic dog as a hunting partner for the purpose of trailing and capturing wild game. As man's methods of hunting developed, the style and type of dog he required was modified and specialized to complement his own hunting abilities. While there is no doubt that prehistoric man depended heavily upon hunting success for his very survival, civilization gradually advanced to the point where hunting became, instead, a sporting pastime of the wealthy aristocracy.

What's in a Name?

Hare hunting with small hounds was popular in England as early as the fourteenth century, and while these hounds were likely of Beagle type, that breed name was not yet in use. The actual origin of the name "Beagle" is uncertain. It may have been derived from the old French *bégeule*, meaning "gape throat" and referring to the baying voice of the hounds when in hot pursuit of their quarry. It has also been often suggested

Beagles are the smallest of English hunting hounds.

that the term refers to the diminutive size of the hound, possibly deriving from the Old English *begele*, or perhaps the Celtic *beag*, both of which mean small. The first known mention of Beagles by name in the English literature can be found in the *Esquire of Low Degree*, published in 1475.

Bewick's *Quadrupeds* (1790) provides us with a most insightful quote regarding the purpose and talents of the Beagle breed. The Beagle is declared to be the smallest of English hounds kept for the chase, and "is only used in hunting the hare; although far inferior in point of speed to that animal, they follow by the exquisiteness of their scent, and trace her foot steps through all her various windings with such exactness and perseverance, that they afford most excellent diversion, and generally reward the hunter's toil with the death of the wearied fugitive. Their tones are soft and musical, and add greatly to the pleasures of the chase."

Varieties

Primary development of the Beagle breed occurred in Britain. English Beagles of the past were comprised of several distinctive varieties, and to this day the hounds of the individual British hunting packs vary somewhat as to size and style.

Mention of the popularity of Beagles, both rough and smooth, in several countries is heralded in the *Sportsman's Cabinet* (1904), and there were reportedly rough-coated Welsh Beagles of excellent type still in existence throughout the early 1900s. Roughs were even documented as

Rabbit hunting with smooth- and rough-coated hounds. Salon De, 1892.

having made an appearance at the Peterborough hound show as recently as 1969, although it is questionable whether the rough-coated type continues to occur among our purebred Beagles today.

Stonehenge, in his fifth edition of the *Manual of British Sports* (1861), divides the breed into four distinctive varieties:

1. the medium Beagle, which may be heavy and Southern-like, or light-boned and Northern-like
2. the dwarf or lapdog Beagle
3. the fox Beagle, which resembles the Foxhound in all but size and dash
4. the rough-coated or terrier Beagle.

The *Essays on Hunting*, penned by an unknown mid-eighteenth-century author, speaks of two very distinct types of hare-hunting hounds, the slow, ponderous, long-eared Southern hound and the North country Beagle, which is described as nimble and vigorous.

Decline in Popularity

While the little Beagles of the Elizabethan period were persistent pack hunters, possessed of great stamina and keen noses, they were lacking somewhat in speed and dash, and failed to remain in favor very long. During the mid-eighteenth century, foxhunting was growing in popularity among those who wished to pursue a more exhilarating sport than watching hounds puzzle out the intricate mazes of the hare. Beagle packs frequently fell into the possession of gentlemen whose age or infirmities prevented their participation in the more strenuous forms of sporting excursions. Beagling was also well suited to the less wealthy, who did not possess horses but could readily keep up with a pack of these smaller hounds on foot.

Paget (1923) remarks that the breed was in great danger of disappearing entirely from England by the close of the eighteenth century. We are greatly indebted to the farmers and landowners of the Southern counties who maintained small packs of Beagles for the purpose of driving rabbits to the gun; otherwise, the valuable bloodlines of earlier packs might have been forever lost. Hounds from sources such as these, in parts of Ireland, Sussex, and the Welsh hills, became impor-

The Warrington Foot Beagles, an organized pack, appear in this photo.

tant foundation stock when the revival in the sport of beagling commenced.

The Revival

A revival of interest in hunting with Beagles began around 1830; the Reverend Phillip Honeywood is credited with being the chief pioneer. By 1886–1887, there were some 18 established Beagle packs, and by 1895 no fewer than 44 packs were hunting in the U.K. Bryden (1902) records that during the 1902–1903 season there were 50 active Beagle packs in the U.K., primarily in England. He lauds the revival of the Beagle for hunting purposes over the previous 20 years, noting that it seemed that just 70 or 80 years prior to that time the breed was nearly lost. It was around this same encouraging time in the history of the Beagle that interest in the breed was beginning to blossom in America.

Development of American Beagling

The first surviving mention of the Beagle (by that name) in America occurs in the town records of Ipswich, Massachusetts, in 1642. *The American Book of the Dog*, edited by G. O. Shields (1891), describes the increased popularity of the Beagle as an American hunting dog due in part to the plentiful supply of small game. Prior to the Civil War, hunters in the Southern states frequently used small hounds, some of which were referred to as Beagles, in pursuit of the fox and hare. However,

these hounds tended to more closely resemble the Dachshund or Basset Hound in type, possessing short legs and weak heads.

Most of the foundation hounds of the breed in this country were imported from the finest British hunting packs. These were truly *dual-purpose* Beagles, possessing both correct conformation and field abilities. The first definite operations of which there is record credit General Richard Rowett of Carlinville, Illinois, as being one of the earliest importers of Beagles, during the 1870s. These hounds were known for their uniform type and bench-show quality of conformation combined with remarkable field ability. It is beyond the scope of a general training book such as this to document the many influential breeding programs and outstanding hounds that contributed to the development of our modern-day Beagle. Entire volumes have been devoted to the subject, and those with an interest in studying the breed history further are encouraged to explore the titles provided in Useful Addresses and Literature, page 142.

Organized Beagling

The American English Beagle Club was established in 1884. The efforts of this group were directed primarily at improving Beagle breed type for show purposes. They were successful in inspiring Beagle breeders of that time to improve the quality of conformation of their hounds and gained recognition of the breed at the shows held by the various all-breed kennel clubs.

Institute Farm—home of the National Beagle Club of America.

In 1890 the National Beagle Club was formed, and held the first Beagle field trial event at Hyannis, Massachusetts, in November of that year. The main objective of the NBC was the sponsorship of Beagle field trials for the purpose of improving hunting qualities, as well as improvement of breed type. In 1891 the American Beagle Club, as it was then known, merged with the NBC to become the National Beagle Club of America, and has been recognized ever since by the American Kennel Club as the parent club of the breed in this country. Organized as a specialty club, the NBC continues today to be committed to improvement of the Beagle on the bench as well as in the field.

In 1916 the Institute Corporation was formed in order to purchase the 400-acre Institute Farm, located in Aldie, Virginia, as a home for NBC activities. This historic wooded property had once been part of Oak Hill, the home of American president James Monroe. Still present today is the three-and-a-half-story stone and stucco main building, constructed in 1854 to house the Loudon County Agricultural Institute and Chemical Academy. Institute Farm was placed on the National Registry of Historic Places and Virginia Landmarks in 1981, and continues to serve as a most excellent running grounds for pack and field activities, including the trials for NBC-registered foot packs of Beagles and Bassets.

The Beagle Advisory Committee of the AKC was formed in 1936 and was responsible for reviewing the growing number of applications for new Beagle clubs, and proposed changes to the rules and regulations for holding field trial events. By the mid-1940s, American Beagling was thriving and had expanded to include nearly 140 active, recognized Beagle clubs.

Desirable Characteristics of the Beagle

Paget describes the desirable traits of the Beagle quite well when he remarks that they "should have the nose to pick out the coldest scent and the drive to carry it on; pace and stamina for the longest day; a constitution capable of withstanding wet and cold; and legs, feet and shoulders

Beagles come in a variety of colors and markings.

able to stand the strain of a fast pace over hard ground." *The Beagle Standard with Interpretations* (1929), compiled by I. W. Carrel, states: "...the foremost qualities in these hounds are nose, instinct or disposition, and the will to go on and on." Mr. James McAleer of Sewickly, Pennsylvania, contributes that for field trial purposes one should also select a Beagle with a competitive spirit (1920).

Many of the behaviors and temperamental traits that add up to enable the Beagle to perform his intended duties in the field seem almost contradictory at times. He must have the independence to throw himself, without hesitation, into the thickest of cover in pursuit of his quarry;

yet at the same time he needs to be sufficiently cooperative to contribute to the work of a pack, and tractable enough to follow the bidding of his master. Hundreds of years of selective breeding have resulted in a scenthound possessed with the desire and determination to locate, track, and account for his quarry, along with the intelligence and natural talent to do so in an efficient and accurate manner. However, many of these same traits that contribute to making the Beagle such a talented hunting companion are often viewed less favorably in his role as a family pet; determination to pursue his inherited instincts is often viewed instead as stubbornness and a lack of trainability.

3 Selection

Before You Get a Dog...

You have come to the decision that the time is right to add a new canine companion to your household—and what could possibly be more appealing than a little Beagle puppy? But before you rush out the door and straight to the nearest litter of baby Beagles, we urge you to slow down and give your potential purchase some serious thought.

Owning a dog requires a long-term commitment, one that should never be entered into lightly. In this day of "disposable dogs," far too many are abandoned into the shelters and rescue programs as a result of impulse purchases that did not work out. As you prepare to enter into a 10-to-15-year relationship with your new Beagle companion, there are a number of factors that should be carefully weighed and considered.

Are You Ready?

The first thing to think about when contemplating the purchase of a dog is why you would like to own one. Purebred dogs, and Beagles in particular, have earned a well-deserved popularity as family companion animals. They are adaptable, faithful comrades that provide their owners with a lifetime of unconditional love and admiration. But dogs are also totally dependent on their owners to provide proper care and training, especially during the difficult times of infirmity and old age.

1. Make sure that the entire family is ready to share their hearts and homes with this merry little hound, and to make the necessary commitment of time and money. The purchase price of your new Beagle is only the tip of the iceberg in terms of financial expenditures; proper maintenance will also require providing a quality diet and safe lodging, along with regular veterinary visits at least once per year.

2. Think about timing. Is this an appropriate time to take on the challenge of training and integrating your new puppy into the household? Beagles find a sense of security in routine. Consistency also is particularly important to successfully housebreaking and training your Beagle. Try to avoid bringing a new puppy into the home during the confusion of the Christmas holidays, or immediately prior to a planned family

vacation. Instead wait until a relatively quiet time, when the family has returned to its normal routine, and preferably when at least one family member can be home all day to provide adequate supervision.

Selecting the Right Type

When selecting the breed of dog best suited to your personal situation and expectations, it is important to understand the purpose for which the breed was originally developed. Talk with breeders and owners and be sure you fully comprehend the natural behaviors and temperament of the Beagle, and are confident that this enthusiastic little scent-hound is the right choice for your family.

What could possibly be cuter?

Gender

Spaying/neutering. Both male and female Beagles can be equally pleasant family companions. If you are acquiring your new hound primarily as a pet, and have no aspirations of his becoming a future star of conformation or field trial competitions, it is highly recommended that you spay/neuter your companion animal. Neutering your Beagle at an early age contributes to the health and well-being of your pet and also effectively eliminates any chance of an accidental breeding. And with the elimination of the associated hormonal influences, there are often fewer gender-related differences in behavior.

The neutered Beagle can participate in Therapy work, Obedience, Tracking, Agility, and junior showmanship competitions, but is not eligible for competition in conformation classes or field trials. If you do chose to keep an unspayed female Beagle, you will need to be prepared to cope with her biannual heat cycle. A typical estrus cycle lasts approximately 21 to 27 days, during which time the female canine produces a bloody discharge, will be attractive to male dogs, and also becomes receptive to breeding. Your normally sweet-natured little lady may also experience distinct mood swings while in heat.

Male dogs, neutered or not, typically lift their leg to urinate or scent-mark their territory; this can take its toll on your

Personality is not dependent on gender.

ornamental plantings and shrubbery. Female Beagles will also scent-mark, but more commonly squat during urination. Unaltered male dogs may occasionally exhibit a tendency to roam in search of mates, or become more aggressive in the presence of another male.

Personality and temperament. These tend to be dependent more on individual differences and inherent influences than on the gender of your Beagle. It is not unusual to find females that are just as dominant and assertive as any male might be, or a male dog that is exceedingly gentle and affectionate. If becoming a breeder is your eventual goal, then the choice of which gender to purchase is obvious. It is the owner of the female who makes all of the breeding decisions, whelps and raises the resulting puppies, and is recognized by the AKC as the breeder of a litter. It is worthy of note, however, that the purchase of a promising

male puppy can have its advantages. Training, conditioning, and showing the dog provide a valuable learning experience while you are waiting for that ideal foundation female to become available.

Puppy or Adult?

The initial impulse of most potential Beagle owners is that they want a puppy, and the younger the better. But there are a number of reasons why it could be to your advantage to consider opening your heart and home to a more mature hound. For the most part, what you see is what you get; with an adult dog you can more accurately evaluate temperament, size, conformation, hunting abilities, and health. It is also more likely that the mature Beagle has received at least some basic manners training and socialization. And since there is less of a demand for adults, they do not often command as high a price as the cute puppy.

The puppy. Selecting a puppy versus an adult makes it more difficult to predict what the future will hold. It typically means you will need to spend a lot more time training and socializing your Beagle, and must endure the sometimes difficult stages of teething, chewing, adolescent exuberance, and frequent veterinarian visits for vaccinations and wormings. Certain hereditary health defects may not surface until one or two years of age and can be heartbreaking. And due to the demand for well-bred puppies, many reputable breeders will have a long waiting list of prospective buyers.

But by choosing a puppy, you have the potential opportunity to shape its personality and manners more so than with an adult hound. Your little Beagle will be the product in part of his genetic background, but also is highly influenced by his surroundings and experiences. Provide a secure and loving home coupled with gentle, consistent training, and your puppy is likely to mature into a well-mannered, confident family companion. If you are prepared to devote the extra effort to training and socializing your Beagle during the formative period of the first year of life, a puppy may be the right choice for you.

The older puppy or adult. If you decide to purchase a puppy, the best age at which to obtain your Beagle must be considered. If you are selecting a Beagle with a specific purpose in mind, such as conformation shows, hunting, or field trial competitions, then it may well be to your advantage to look for an older puppy or adult Beagle, where quality is less in question. For the family companion, eight to ten weeks is a good age at which to introduce your puppy to his new home. Prior to seven weeks, it is important for puppies to remain with their littermates in order to develop appropriate bonds and learn how to interact with other canines. By two months of age, puppies will be better prepared both mentally and physically to make their way in the world. An eight-week-old puppy from a reputable source will also have received an initial series of protective vaccinations and wormings prior to placement.

An older puppy can also prove to be a fine companion, and is still impressionable enough for you to affect his future personality, but you will want to make sure that he has been properly socialized and

How do I choose just one?

Puppies are typically a reflection of their parents.

handled frequently by humans. The critical period for socialization and bonding with humans extends from shortly after birth through about three months of age; a puppy raised without human companionship during this time may experience more difficulty bonding with his new family.

Consider the Source

A knowledgeable breeder is typically the best source from which to consider purchasing your Beagle. Reputable, responsible breeders are devoted to their chosen breed and carefully plan each litter with an eye toward emphasizing the positive traits and eliminating faults. Their goal is to produce only mentally and physically sound animals that are a credit to their breed.

Another good reason to buy directly from a breeder is that you will have the opportunity to meet and interact with the mother of the puppies, and very often the sire or other close relatives as well. From these adult hounds you can gain a pretty fair impression of what your puppy will be like at maturity. And buying from a responsible breeder is much like becoming part of an extended family—the breeder will be there to provide much needed guidance and support through the difficult times, and also to share in the joy of your successes.

Breed Rescues and Shelters

Another excellent source for both older puppies and adult Beagles is through the organized Beagle rescue programs. The hounds in these rescue programs are there for a variety of reasons, often through no fault of their own. Generally speaking, the majority of hounds accepted into Beagle rescue range in age from puppies through three years old; they are of sound temperament and in good health. Once accepted into the program, the hounds are usually spayed/neutered, receive appropriate health care, and may be placed into a foster home where they receive further socialization and basic manners training (see page 143 for rescue contacts).

Pet Shops and Puppy Mills

The current trend in retail pet shops seems to be moving away from the actual sale of puppies and kittens. Pet supply stores frequently restrict their live animal sales to aquarium-type pets, such as fish, reptiles, and smaller mammals. Many stores now support the adoption of cats and dogs from humane shelters and rescue organizations as an alternative to the sale of purebred puppies. But you may find a pet shop in your area that does still deal in purebred dogs, and happens to have a Beagle puppy available. Purchasing a Beagle from a retail vendor is in some ways similar to adopting a rescued hound when it comes to the amount of background information you are likely to receive. In most cases you will know little more than the breed, age, and gender of your puppy prior to purchase. There is no opportunity to visit with the pup's parents or talk with the breeder; you also will not know the hereditary tendencies of the bloodlines.

Note: Adopting a Beagle from a shelter leaves a few more unanswered questions, but if you are not as concerned about knowing your pet's lineage and background, a hound from such a source can still be a fine companion. You will want to take your time and evaluate the personality and behavior patterns of the shelter dog as best as possible. If it was turned in by the previous owners, attempt to contact them and find out the reason. If they gave the hound up due to a biting incident, or because of an expensive or serious medical problem, you would want to know. However, these situations are rare, and the majority of Beagles found in shelters are there because a previous owner simply did not have the time or commitment to provide adequate training.

If you do choose to consider a pet shop puppy, be sure to avoid impulse buying. Follow the same procedures for evaluating the health and temperament of your future companion as you would when visiting a Beagle breeder (see page 21). Also ask to read through the written sales agreement, and make sure that it includes a health guarantee and terms that you find acceptable.

Purchasing a Beagle from a puppy mill operation should be avoided at all costs! Puppy mill establishments typically produce litters of a variety of popular breeds en masse, solely for the purpose of financial profit. Dogs are often housed in crowded pens containing multiple females; they may be kept in unsanitary conditions, with little attention given to health or socialization. Since there is rarely any effort to screen potential breeding animals for hereditary faults, and the dogs receive only minimal care, the resulting puppies are often of poor quality and questionable temperament.

Locating a Responsible Breeder

One of the best methods for locating a reputable breeder from which to purchase your puppy is through referrals made by friends, acquaintances, or your veterinarian. You may also want to attend a local dog show or Beagle field trial, and talk to owners and handlers, though as a courtesy, please refrain from doing so immediately before or while their hound is competing. You might even contact the AKC to obtain the names and addresses of Beagle or all-breed clubs that could provide breeder referrals within your home area.

You can also locate breeders through an Internet search, advertisements in beagling magazines, or through the classifieds of your local newspaper. The listing of potentially useful addresses and web sites in this book should be helpful as well (see page 142).

Whichever method you use, it is important to remember that not all Beagle breeders are alike: Some are highly ethical and selectively breed to produce the best-quality puppies they possibly can; others are less interested in the quality of the

puppies than in how much profit they can potentially sell them for. You will need to do your homework, ask questions, and judge for yourself which breeders represent a good, responsible source from which to purchase your Beagle.

In order to make a well-informed choice, learn as much as you can about the Beagle breed before you go to look at litters of puppies. Review the breed standard, and make sure you are also familiar with common health problems in the breed, and what constitutes correct temperament. (You can learn more about potential health concerns, such as epilepsy and disc disease, by visiting the NBC web site.) A responsible breeder should show evidence of knowledge and serious involvement with the breed, and be willing to openly answer your questions and discuss the potential problems and requirements associated with Beagle ownership. Price alone should not be a major factor in your decision; the original purchase price of a puppy matters little when averaged over the lifetime of your Beagle.

Think Purpose

The purpose for which you are obtaining a Beagle will play an important role in determining the source from which you should make your eventual purchase. If your goal is no more than to locate a pleasant family companion, then a healthy, well-adjusted puppy from any reputable breeder may suffice. But if your goal is to own a good prospect for exhibition at the conformation shows, an efficient hunting hound, or a competitive field trial Beagle, then you will need to further narrow the search for the best possible source.

Dog Show Prospect

If you think that you might find the experience of competing with your hound at the AKC dog shows enjoyable, you should explore the possibilities prior to committing to a purchase. If indeed you have the time, motivation, and financial means to launch a show career, you will want to contact successful breeders of conformation and/or Obedience Beagles. The best possible source for a future show prospect will be an experienced breeder who regularly competes at the dog shows and wins with some consistency. Keep in mind that even in a litter from an outstanding pedigree and where both parents are champions, not every puppy can be guaranteed to be an excellent show prospect, but your chances of success will at least be greatly improved.

Hunting and Field Trial

Likewise, if you want your Beagle to be a faithful and efficient hunting companion, you should seek out a breeder who produces hounds primarily for the sport of hunting small game. If successful competition at the field trials is your goal, then again you need to narrow the possibilities to kennels that have a history of producing top field winners in both the style of trial format you prefer and within your general area of the country. There is a great deal

Pictured is a handsome show prospect.

of difference between Beagles produced for the current Brace format field trials, and those bred for Small Pack Option or Large Pack on Hare events. Again, not every puppy in a litter from good field breeding is necessarily going to live up to expectations, but your chances are better if you select the source carefully.

How Do You Choose?

The appointed day has finally come, you have located a reputable source of quality puppies, and you are now faced with making a selection of which pup to take home. You may find yourself confronted by the difficult task of choosing from among a vigorous litter where all puppies appear equally affectionate and healthy. But with closer, individual examination, even the novice should be capable of detecting differences in soundness, conformation, and personality.

The Parents

A quality puppy of even temperament is often a reflection of its parents. You should be able to meet and examine the mother of the puppies, and preferably the sire or other close relatives as well. If the sire is not present, ask to see a photo and any available information regarding his competition record and health. Review the pedigree as well; if the parents and numerous other ancestors have earned titles in show or performance events, this gives you some idea of the potential qualities of their offspring.

Good health is a prerequisite.

Do not be dismayed if the physical appearance of the mother is less than impressive. She has just been through approximately two months of pregnancy followed by the nutritional drain of nursing the litter. Following weaning, her udders and abdomen may continue to sag for several months, and hormonal changes often result in a dry, shedding coat. She may be thin from the effort, or possibly overweight if the breeder has overindulged her with a high-quality growth formula feed. In any case, despite her appearance, the dam should be friendly and sociable and representative of proper Beagle type.

The Litter

Before you proceed further, take a moment to stand back and look at the entire litter. Are the surroundings clean and well kept? Puppies can make a mess of a room quickly, but you should not see traces of spoiled food, old feces, or other signs of poor sanitation and neglect. If there are fresh stools, do they look healthy and well formed? Or are they soft, full of worms, or otherwise indicative of problems? You do not want to select a puppy from an unhealthy litter; all of the pups should appear robust and well cared for.

Observe the puppies as they play together and interact. This should help you to determine the more dominant or submissive individuals, which are followers, and which are more assertive or independent. Your personal situation, expectations, and training abilities will determine which personality type is best for you. Approach the litter, speaking to the puppies in a soft voice. Make note of which puppies immediately run to greet you, tails wagging, whining for further attention; also take notice of any that hang back or attempt to retreat to a secure hiding place.

Physical Examination

If one particular puppy catches your eye, gently lift him out of the pen and examine him head on.

■ Eyes should be bright and clear, with no visible cloudy spots. Injuries, cataracts, or other imperfections could interfere with vision. If the third eyelid is swollen or inflamed, it could indicate infection; if there is a large red bulge located at the inner corner of the eye, the puppy has *cherry eye*, and may require surgery to correct the problem by tacking the irritated gland back into place.

■ The nose should be cool and moist. There should be no noticeable wheezing or other noises when the puppy breathes. Also be wary of a coughing puppy, as this could be an indication of *kennel cough*, an upper-respiratory condition.

■ The teeth should preferably meet in a scissors or level bite. If the teeth extend out noticeably further on the top jaw (overshot) or the bottom jaw juts forward (undershot), this would detract from the show potential of the hound, and if severe enough could affect future health.

■ Beagle ears are an area of particular concern. The earflap should be well covered with hair, and not crusty or covered with scabs, though due to roughhousing with littermates, a Beagle puppy may have evidence of a few prior nips on the ears. Examine the ear canal; it should be clean and sweet smelling. If there is a foul odor, damp discharge, or heavy buildup of wax and debris, the puppy likely has an infection or ear mite infestation. Also watch for scratching and head shaking as possible indications of trouble.

■ Now, as you sit on the floor, carefully roll the puppy belly up onto your lap. If he is of even temperament and used to being handled he should protest only momentarily and then quiet down. Examine the abdomen; it should be smooth, clean, and healthy looking. If there is an excess of scabs and pimples, chances are the litter has been housed in unsanitary conditions. A bulging naval probably indicates an umbilical hernia. Unless it is severe, it causes the puppy little harm and is easily corrected by minor surgery, often done at the same time as the spay/neuter procedure.

■ Male puppies should be scrutinized to be sure that they possess two normal testicles fully descended into the scrotum. If one or both cannot be located and are suspected to be undescended, the dog is undesirable for competition or breeding purposes and neutering is highly recommended for health reasons. Check female puppies for pasting or discharge around the vulva, which could indicate a vaginal or urinary tract infection.

■ The hair around the anal area should be clean and free from any signs of worms or diarrhea.

- The coat should be shiny and healthy looking; a brittle, dry hair coat or bare, scabby areas and irritated skin may be the result of lice, mites, or other parasitic infestation.

Whether your Beagle has a future as a potential show star, Obedience, Agility, or field trial competitor, or simply an occasional hunting companion, you will next want to evaluate the pup for soundness of structure and correct conformation. At eight to ten weeks of age, a Beagle puppy should appear similar to the adult hound in miniature. He should move with a smooth and easy gait, never limping, hitching, or with legs wobbling this way and that. When the puppy stands, he should be well balanced in appearance, with straight legs, level topline, and nicely sloping shoulders and knees. If you are looking for a future conformation show prospect, go over the pup point by point, comparing him to the ideal described in the breed standard (see Chapter 15).

Evaluating Temperament

You should already have an initial impression about the puppy's individual personality based on your observations of litter interactions. When you first reached for him to lift him out of the pen for examination, he should have been wriggling with excitement at the prospect of your undivided attention. If instead he cowered away in fear, snapped, and growled or cried, he may well be a poor candidate for either competition or family companionship purposes.

- Sit down or kneel, placing the puppy beside you on the floor, and try to engage him in play. Show him a small squeaky toy or ball, then gently toss the toy a short distance and watch his reaction. If he shows an interest in interacting with you and chases the toy, possibly retrieving it and bringing it back to you for another game, he

Even-tempered puppies grow into well-mannered adults.

shows promise for future training and bonding with his human family.

■ Clap your hands or otherwise create a sudden noise, and watch the puppy's reaction. He may initially be startled, but should quickly ascertain that all is well and return to a stance of tail up and wagging. If instead he tucks his tail, runs, and hides, he may be overly submissive and sensitive to noises—not a good sign if you want to be able to take your Beagle out in public, go hunting, or participate in competition events.

■ Stand up and begin to walk away from the puppy, clucking or calling to him softly. A dominant puppy will follow readily, tail up and underfoot; a more submissive puppy might be a little more hesitant, but should still follow. If he runs away, he may be easily distracted and more difficult to train, or perhaps is just plain shy.

■ Again pick up the puppy and hold him securely, but suspended momentarily in the air. Then place him belly up on your lap and hold him there for a few seconds. In both cases, the very dominant puppy will squirm and struggle fiercely to escape; dominant puppies are best suited to an adult situation, are especially outgoing, and are typically intelligent, but can be a bit more challenging to train. The more settled puppy will possibly struggle initially, then gradually accept the restraint; this type of puppy should still be self-confident enough to perform well in competition events, and is likely to be a quick learner that will fit comfortably into a family situation. The puppy that shows no resistance, immedi-

Let's play!

ately accepting the situation and licking your hands is more submissive; the submissive puppy, so long as it is not taken to the extreme of being shy, can potentially be an excellent choice for an older couple or family with small children.

■ Finally, take your chosen puppy into another room or outdoors, away from the security of his littermates and familiar surroundings. Set him down next to you on the ground and talk to him reassuringly while petting him or scratching gently behind the ears. If he reacts confidently, and responds to your attentions with puppy kisses and a wagging tail, your selection may well be made.

Making the Commitment

Before you conclude the purchase, there are a few more matters to attend to.

Health Records

Ask the breeder to go over the pup's health records with you. Records should include a list of all vaccinations and wormings that have been administered and by whom, what products were used, and the dates received. Also included should be notes regarding any health problems encountered, treatments provided, and dates on which future vaccinations or treatments are due. If the puppy is currently receiving medication for any

This puppy readily accepts gentle restraint.

sort of ailment, the breeder should be willing to hold the puppy for you until all treatments have been completed. If the puppy has been started on heartworm preventative, the product used and dates should also be noted.

Feeding. If you have not already done so, ask the breeder what brand and variety of puppy food the litter has been eating, the amount you should offer your puppy, and the frequency and schedule of feeding. You will want to make any dietary changes gradually, in order to avoid unnecessary stress and digestive upsets.

Registration and Sales Agreement

If the litter has been registered with the American Kennel Club, or other major registry of purebred dogs, you should receive a registration application with the purchase of your Beagle. This document should be completed and signed by both the litter owner and you, the new owner. Registration will allow you to enter your Beagle for competition in dog events, and to potentially be used for breeding purposes to produce a litter of registerable, purebred puppies.

You will notice on the AKC registration application an area where the breeder must select either *full* or *limited* registration for this puppy. If the *limited* registration option has been marked, it means that in the opinion of the breeder, this particular puppy demonstrates some trait that they do not wish to see perpetuated; it could be something as minor as the way the hound carries his tail. Limited registration does not in any way indicate that you are somehow getting a defective animal, and such a pup is otherwise likely to be an outstanding pet. But you must remember that limited registration means *not for breeding purposes* and a Beagle on limited registration is ineligible to compete in the conformation show classes or licensed field trial events. Any future offspring of a dog that is placed on limited registration could not be registered with the AKC.

All health guarantees and other agreements regarding the purchase should be clearly stated in a written sales contract. You can expect the written sales agreement from a responsible breeder to include a clause requiring that the puppy be examined by your veterinarian within a few days of purchase. If the pup is found to be ill at that time, the agreement will outline terms for either refund or replacement of the hound. It is not unreasonable for the breeder to also include requirements that the Beagle receive proper care and housing, and to sell pet puppies—those on limited registration—with a spay/neuter agreement that requires their sterilization by a specified age. Many sellers will add to the

> **Note:** In this and subsequent chapters we will, for ease of communication, be referring to your new Beagle by the name "Bailey," and using masculine pronouns in most situations. No sexism is intended.

agreement a *responsible breeder clause* that requires that the dog be returned to the breeder for rehoming if at any point in its lifetime you are unable to or decide not to keep it. Reputable breeders prefer to take responsibility for the dogs they produce, and do not want to risk their ending up in a bad situation or dumped into a shelter or rescue program.

Heading Home

If all is in order, and you are happy with your selection, then the time has come to sign the paperwork and conclude your purchase. You may now place Bailey safely in his crate for the car ride home. This is where the hard work really begins, but if you have chosen to own a Beagle for all the right reasons, it will be a labor of love.

4 Foundations of Training

Early Socialization

Scientific studies have established that the experiences during the first few months of a puppy's life will have a profound and lasting impact on his adult temperament and behavior. Your Beagle's personality will have been strongly influenced by prior interactions with his mother and littermates, as well as the socialization and environment provided by his breeder. If you are bringing Bailey into your home within the first 12 to 16 weeks of his life, you also will be responsible for an important portion of his early social development.

Mom provides for all neonatal needs.

Socialization. This can be defined as the process through which a puppy develops interactive skills with other canines and humans, and learns how to respond confidently to different situations and environmental influences. During Bailey's puppyhood, he will progress through a number of distinct stages of development that will play a critical role in shaping his adult social behaviors.

The Canine Pack

From birth through the age of approximately six weeks, a puppy learns the rules of proper canine social interaction and how to relate to other members of his own species. Puppies that are removed from the litter environment too soon will typically have difficulty interacting with other dogs when mature. Within the warm, secure environment of the whelping box, his mother provides for all of the puppy's basic, neonatal needs. She will also furnish early lessons in discipline when the puppy's behavior exceeds acceptable limits.

As his senses and motor skills develop, the puppy begins to explore his environment. He learns to communicate through vocalizations and body posture, and begins to interact socially with littermates.

Play and minor skirmishes teach the puppy about dominance and submission, and how to use the correct behavioral response for the situation at hand. Puppies may also begin to develop an initial impression of humans during this stage, but the more critical period of human socialization will not begin until closer to seven weeks of age.

- Birth to two weeks is the neonatal period. During this stage the puppies do little more than eat and sleep. They are unable to see, hear, regulate their own body temperature, or eliminate without their mother's stimulation. Young puppies do, however, respond to tactile stimulation, are able to distinguish scents, and are aware of direct contact. They respond positively to gentle caressing and handling, which has been shown to stimulate increased brain development.

- Two to three weeks of age is an important transition period. At 10 days the pups' eyes will begin to open, as do the ears, and by about 14 days puppies will begin to see and hear. As they receive additionally sensory input, exposure to a variety of different textures, sounds, and scents helps puppies learn how to respond to environmental variation. If the breeder continues to handle each puppy daily, speaking softly and giving them individual attention, this lays the foundation for future bonding with humans.

- Twenty-one to twenty-three days is the critical awareness period. It is a time of rapid sensory development, and it is important that radical changes in environment be avoided during this stage.

- At three to six weeks the puppy reaches the peak of the canine socialization period. He takes his first wobbly steps and will soon begin to wrestle and play more actively with his littermates. This is the stage at which the brain is suddenly receiving a multitude of messages and the puppy now has the ability to learn. It is particularly important for the puppies to remain with their mother and littermates during this time period; they are learning the etiquette of canine interaction and that they are dogs. The influence of their mother will aid in shaping sibling interactions and the puppy learns to avoid his mother's discipline by acting submissively. Milk teeth are erupting, and supplementation of the puppies' diet is begun, but the litter is not yet fully weaned.

Human Socialization

The human socialization period is from the seventh through about the twelfth week, with the experiences and education received by the puppy pretty much establishing his character by sixteen weeks of age. At this stage the puppy is now ready to transfer his affections and dependence from his mother to his people. If possible, this is an ideal time to incorporate Bailey into his new household. These first few weeks in his new home will be among the most important in the socialization process.

- From five to seven weeks of age, all good breeders will have begun to encourage their puppies to trust and interact with people. Once protected by their initial vaccinations, puppies are introduced to the outdoors and

Five-week-old puppies are very social.

permitted to meet other friendly canines, new adults, and children. Most reputable breeders will try to expose their puppies to a variety of stimulating environments and situations. Short periods of simple training may have been started, and agility of movement encouraged. All of this helps in building the puppy's confidence and fosters the process of bonding with humans.

■ Seven to ten weeks is an exciting stage in your puppy's development. He is now fully weaned and neurologically complete. If you are bringing Bailey home now, it is important to remember that he is still continuing to develop social patterns and behavior. Try to keep his schedule full for the first few days, being sure to abide by the *house rules* and establishing good manners right from the start. During this critical stage, some puppies will experience what is referred to as a *fear period*; they may lose some of their

former self-confidence and seem apprehensive in certain situations. This has little to do with separation from their mother or siblings. Try to avoid traumatic experiences during this period, providing instead controlled activities and gentle play training. With your careful guidance and affections, Bailey should come through just fine and at twelve weeks will be on the threshold of acceptable behavior.

■ By twelve weeks of age, well-socialized puppies are again confidently tackling new experiences, and boldly approaching people and other animals. If they are still in the breeder's household, puppies need to be separated into individual living quarters. Competition between littermates becomes more intense, and one puppy may exert his dominance at the expense of the personalities of the others. This is the period during which Bailey is developing his independence and self-confidence. It is also a time during which you will want to be sure to establish in his mind that you are his pack leader. All tests of strength between human and puppy (such as tug-of-war) should be discontinued and behaviors such as chewing on hands, hair, or clothing discouraged. Continue bonding and interacting with Bailey in a positive manner, and by four months of age his personality will be fully set as a well-socialized, pleasant Beagle companion.

Bonding with Your Beagle

From the moment of picking Bailey up at the breeder's, you began to form a relationship that will be the basis of your life together. Now that you have brought him home, what should you do first to help him become a productive member of the household?

During the earliest stages of training, you will want Bailey to bond with you and establish a reciprocal trust. It is also important that he learn his position as a subordinate member of the family and respectfully look to you as his pack leader for guidance. By having all members of the family participate in some simple bonding exercises, you will minimize the potential for inappropriate behavior patterns later, such as aggression or extreme dominance.

■ While Bailey is still small, handle him often. Carefully pick him up for a few moments, and then praise and release him only after he has stopped strug-

Note: Until your Beagle puppy has completed a series of protective vaccinations at 12 to 16 weeks of age, he remains vulnerable to infectious disease. Avoid exposure to any canines of unknown health history during this time period. The specific types of vaccines, and recommended schedule for administration, are dependent upon the risks within your home area. Please follow your veterinarian's recommendations regarding the best preventive health care program for your hound.

Playtime is part of the bonding process.

gling and relaxes in acceptance. Gently but firmly hold him on your lap, and then, using moderate pressure, pet or brush his head, body, and legs. He should become comfortable with your handling his feet and ears particularly, as these are areas that will require frequent grooming.

■ Encourage constructive play, such as retrieving a small toy. Most Beagle pups will enjoy a game of *Fetch* immensely, and quickly learn that only by returning the toy to you will the interactive fun continue. Likewise, teach Bailey to relinquish toys or objects on command, and do not engage in tug-of-war.

■ Never allow Bailey to stand on or over you during play; you want him to look up to you as the dominant individual in your relationship. This is just one of several situations where an under-

Mother teaches lessons in dominance and submission.

standing of how dominant and submissive canines interact can assist you in your training. Occasionally look Bailey in the eye until he looks away; the one who holds eye contact longest is *alpha* (the more dominant individual). Another demonstration of dominance that you can use is what some trainers call the *nose hug*: When you greet Bailey, gently cup his muzzle in your hand and give it a firm shake.

■ Bailey should always be fed only after you have yourself finished eating. From the very start, adult family members should practice taking the puppy's food dish away during mealtime; do this several times each week. Beagles in general have a tendency to become very food possessive, and a Beagle that guards his food can become inappropriately aggressive. Remove the food bowl for a few moments, and then deposit a delicious tidbit before returning it to the puppy to finish his meal in peace. Bailey should learn that your presence in the vicinity of his food bowl is to his benefit.

■ Once Bailey has mastered a simple obedience exercise, such as the *sit* (see page 56), ask him to obey that command prior to everyday activities such as being fed, going outside, or playtime. Nothing in life is free.

■ Always praise Bailey for his appropriate behaviors, even those as basic as lying quietly on his dog bed, chewing his rawhide (not your shoes or furniture), and relieving himself in the appropriate outdoor location. Avoid giving him the opportunity to repeatedly make mistakes. Correct but do not punish or physically discipline your puppy. Actions such as swatting Bailey or rubbing his nose in a mess will have a negative impact on his bonding with humans. Beating a dog into submission is not training!

Special tip: You may find it helpful to post a list of the more commonly used commands (such as "Watch me," "Sit," "Come," "Heel," and "Leave it") in a place where everyone in the household can become familiar with them.

Rules of Basic Training

Beginning with the first day you bring Bailey into your home, it is important to remember that he is learning and being trained every minute of the day. So often new owners are of the mistaken impression that *training* their dog takes place only during the actual teaching of formal obedience exercises. But Bailey is an intelligent, perceptive animal that is constantly learning, and while it is easy to establish acceptable behavior patterns during these early months of a relationship, many owners inadvertently teach bad habits without even realizing it.

Consistency Is Key

The most important rule of training is *always be consistent.* It is important not only for the person primarily responsible for Bailey's training to be consistent in his or her actions and use of word commands, but also for the entire family to do the same. For example, if you are teaching Bailey to come to you when using the command *"Bailey, come!"* but another family member calls him using the words *"Here Pup!"* or *"Let's go!"* your Beagle may become quite confused as to

the point you are trying to make. He will learn much more quickly what is expected of him if all family members use the same basic commands at all times.

When you begin training any behavior, be sure to always follow through to the end, and only praise or reward when Bailey responds appropriately. Don't praise him for a failed attempt or inaccurate response, and never before he has completed the exercise; otherwise, your hound may begin to assume that *close* is good enough. If you are inconsistent in what you expect of him, he will likely respond by being equally inconsistent in his reaction to your commands.

Early training. During Bailey's early training, one of the most critical parts of consistency involves the following: *never ask or expect your Beagle to obey a command he does not understand or can evade.* If you cannot control his reaction or enforce appropriate behavior, do not use commands while Bailey is still in the process of being trained. Suppose your little scenthound is off leash and comes across the ultimate distraction for a Beagle—a wild rabbit. He will very likely give in to his natural instincts and give chase. It should be obvious that commanding your

Commonly Used Commands

In order to prevent confusion, and better communicate with your Beagle during training, you need to be consistent in your use of commands. Choose one specific word and use it repeatedly to indicate the desired behavior. When selecting command words, however, you will want to be careful not to misuse a formal obedience command. In situations where a less precise behavior is desired, use an alternate command. Some commonly used commands include the following:

- *"Come"*—A formal obedience recall, in which the dog comes directly to you and sits in front of you, face to face.
- *"Here"* or *"Let's go"*—The informal recall, a more casual command for the dog to make progress in your direction. Often used when hunting when you want your Beagle to move off with you toward a different area.
- *"Sit"*—Used to have your dog assume a sitting position.
- *"Down"*—A completely separate command from the sit; indicates that the dog should lie down on the ground.

- *"Off"*—The command for your dog to stop jumping up; also used to indicate he must remove himself from his current location, such as your living room couch. Do not misuse the term *"Down"* when what you really mean is *"Off."*
- *"Heel"*—Formal obedience exercise in which the dog walks in position beside your left knee and must sit each time you stop moving forward.
- *"Walkies"* or *"Walk"*—Informal but polite walking on leash. Your Beagle should not pull, but should remain within leash range while usually being permitted some freedom to explore.
- *"Stay"*—Formal command indicating that the dog must not move from his current position until you return to his side and release him.
- *"Wait"*—Also indicates that the dog is to hold his current position, but only temporarily; followed by a remote release or recall.
- *"Okay"*—The release command. *"Okay"* indicates to the dog that the exercise is over, and also that praise/rewards are about to follow for a job well done.

untrained Beagle buddy to *"Come!"* in this situation is unlikely to result in the desired behavior. Even worse, your hound has just learned that he can get away with ignoring your commands in situations where you have little physical control. A better reaction would be to go to Bailey

and stop or prevent him from continuing his actions, whenever the current behavior is deemed inappropriate. Or, if he is going to be your future hunting companion and the timing and location are acceptable, you might elect to simply allow him to continue his pursuit of the rabbit.

Reward Correct Behavior

The second rule of a positive approach to basic training is to *always reward your Beagle for correct behavior; do not reward, even unintentionally, for inappropriate behavior.* Assuming that Bailey has learned to respect and admire you as his pack leader, he is also going to have a strong desire to please you and will look to you for guidance. By rewarding his appropriate behaviors, whether by simple praise or the addition of a tasty morsel, you are telling him in no uncertain terms when he has done things right. Early on, you want to try and put Bailey in a position where he can always do right and has few opportunities to make mistakes. This is a skill of dog training that comes naturally to some owners, and for others, must be learned. Praise is important because it indicates to Bailey that you are pleased with and approve of his actions, but care must be taken not to overdo the rewards; a simple word of encouragement, scratching behind the ears, or a small tidbit are fine. Entering into a lavish amount of verbal praise, however, or giving a handful of treats can quickly distract your Beagle's attention from what he has just learned and therefore may fail at reinforcing the desired behavior.

You may be wondering about the previous warning against rewarding incorrect behavior. Why would anyone do that? Obviously you don't want to intentionally encourage Bailey to do anything inappropriate, but without even realizing it many novice owners do just that. In an attempt to comfort or correct their new Beagle, they many times inadvertently reward his unacceptable actions *from the dog's perspective.* One prime example comes to mind—the puppy that cries when placed in his crate. There are few sounds in this world that are sadder or more disturbing than the mournful howl of an eight-week-old puppy protesting the confinement of his crate. Yet the best thing you can possibly do is to totally ignore his pleas for attention. If you go to him and either coddle him with gentle words of comfort, or worse yet, release him from the crate, you have just given him exactly what he wanted—your undivided attention. Likewise, if you go to him and scold his crying, he still has succeeded in gaining your attention and company. To your lonely Beagle baby, even negative attention may seem better than none at all. In either case, the owner has unintentionally rewarded the Beagle's undesirable howling by providing him with exactly what he

Use praise and reward for appropriate behavior.

wanted. Bailey has learned that making a lot of noise is a good thing, and it becomes a behavior he is likely to use more frequently in the future. Beagles are highly intelligent, and given the opportunity, can learn how to manipulate their human companions. Fortunately, they also will quickly abandon those behaviors that are unsuccessful; this is why ignoring inappropriate actions is, in many cases, the best way to curtail them.

Keep Sessions Short

Finally, remember that to be successful you should always keep training sessions short and to the point. Beagles, and dogs in general, tend to have rather short attention spans. Regardless of Bailey's age, you are likely to experience the most success if you limit formal training to sessions of not more than 10 to 15 minutes at a time. You want to try and keep the experience enjoyable for both yourself and Bailey. Longer sessions may cause your hound to become bored and lose interest, after which point nothing further will be learned. When this happens, you are more likely to become frustrated as well. Should you ever lose your temper and lash out, then nothing good will come of the training session and you could negatively impact your relationship with Bailey in the process. Try to set aside short periods of quality time, away from distractions, during which you can concentrate on teaching Bailey appropriate behaviors. Sessions of 10 minutes each day will be far more productive in achieving your goals than a single 60-minute effort once a week.

Because Bailey is constantly learning, there will be plenty of additional opportunities for training apart from these formal sessions. Whenever you observe your Beagle naturally doing something you are trying to train, don't pass up the chance to reinforce the correct behavior. Through consistency and proper use of praise and rewards, your Beagle will soon come to understand what you expect of him and how to respond appropriately to your commands.

Tractability

Tractability is just the professional dog trainer's fancy word for trainability. It is dependent in part on basic breed character as well as on the individual personality of your hound. In general, tractability is a measure of the dog's ability and desire to learn, including how well he focuses on and follows direction from his master. While Beagles tend to be very intelligent and social characters, most obedience trainers will tell you they are not particularly tractable. They often lack the focus and motivation to obey formal obedience commands with the same accuracy and enthusiasm as more tractable breeds, such as Border Collies or Golden Retrievers. Due to the hundreds of years of selective breeding for specific hunting traits, your Beagle is naturally predisposed to be a more independent and creative thinker.

Intelligence

A lesser degree of tractability should not be mistaken for lack of intelligence.

Beagles have an amazing capability for learning and problem solving—and intelligence is defined as just that: the ability to think, and to solve problems. Dogs come in a variety of different types and millions of individual personalities. Specific breeds are not really more or less intelligent than one another so much as they are genetically programmed to learn different tasks with greater or lesser ease.

So when Bailey seems slower to learn his obedience commands than the Golden Retriever puppy next door, it doesn't necessarily mean he is dumb, just a different, more independent type of canine personality. Beagles were bred and developed for their ability to think on their own, often working independently and at some distance from their master while afield. This does not mean your Beagle is going to be impossible to train, just a bit more challenging. You will need to be as creative and quick thinking as Bailey in order to train him well. Try to keep his lessons interesting and challenging, and as always, encourage him to look to you, his alpha, for guidance and approval.

Positive and Negative Reinforcement

Regardless of the specific methods employed, Bailey's basic training will be accomplished through the use of positive and negative reinforcements. Positive reinforcement involves the use of *rewards,* which result in an increase in the selected behavior. Negative reinforcement involves the use of *corrections* and *discipline,* which result in a decrease in the selected behavior. Keep firmly in mind that the terms *correction* and *discipline* should not automatically imply the infliction of physical punishment on your Beagle.

Positive Motivation

Positive reinforcement is one of the most powerful means you can use for shaping or modifying your Beagle's behavior. By providing a pleasant and rewarding stimulus immediately following the desirable behavior, that behavior becomes more likely to be repeated in the future. Correct timing is essential, as Bailey needs to associate the reward with the selected behavior in order for the reinforcement to be effective.

Beagles are extremely motivated by the prospect of receiving food.

Rewards. Rewards can be divided into two categories:

1. *Primary rewards* are those things that are inherently rewarding to your Beagle, and will likely include food items, petting, and a favorite toy or activity.

2. A *secondary reward* is something that the dog has learned to accept as a reward and acknowledgment of proper behavior, such as vocal praise, a click, etc.

As you begin Bailey's training you will probably find it most productive to use primary rewards as motivation in association with secondary rewards. The reward can be anything your hound is highly motivated by; for the typical Beagle pieces of dry kibble or tiny bits of hot dog work well. While a few dogs seem to be motivated by verbal praise, most Beagles must learn to accept praise as a secondary reward through association with something more desirable. Before you assume that this system of positive reinforcement

Note: In order to be effective, corrections must be delivered *while the hound is actually engaged in the undesirable behavior.* Never punish or correct Bailey *after the fact,* as he will have no idea what you are so upset about. The infliction of discipline or punishment delivered too late may leave him feeling assaulted and confused. He is likely to view you as unpredictable and may further react to physical punishment by becoming fearful, distrusting, or even aggressive.

will require you to be forever forced to carry an endless supply of doggie treats in your pocket, let me reassure you this is not the case. Of course, while Bailey is still in the process of learning a new behavior it will be advantageous to reward every correct action, providing continuous reinforcement, but once the behavior has been mastered, intermittent reinforcement should be used. Continue to praise your Beagle each time he performs the desired behavior, but only occasionally reward with a treat or other primary motivator. This actually serves to foster a more consistent response, because Bailey has learned that if he continues to respond with the desired behavior, he will eventually get the reward he enjoys.

Correct and Incorrect Use of Discipline

I'll say it again: *Discipline does not necessarily mean the infliction of physical punishment.* In the vast majority of cases, especially when dealing with a puppy, the best means of correction is through distraction. When you catch Bailey doing something unacceptable, stop him and replace the activity immediately with a positive behavior. Limit your correction to a sharp *"No!"* issued in a tone of voice that mirrors the growl your Beagle's mother might have used when the puppy exhibited a socially unacceptable behavior in the whelping box. When he responds to your correction, and ceases the undesirable behavior to engage in the acceptable action, immediately praise and reward him for listening to you. This will help to enforce the acceptable behavior and also helps build your hound's confidence. An example might be when you catch Bailey enthusiastically gnawing on your new shoe. You left it lying within reach, and he had no way of knowing it was not intended for him. A sharp *"No!"* is sufficient to indicate your displeasure, after which you remove the shoe from his vicinity and substitute an acceptable chew item. When he begins to chew the correct item, praise him for his appropriate behavior.

Punishment. This is rarely the best approach to modifying behavior, and it often creates more problems than it solves. The pitfalls are numerous. Attempted use of punishment might not only fail to curb the intended behavior, but can wipe out desirable behaviors as well. A classic example is the dog that gets loose and does not immediately come when called. When the dog finally does respond and return to the master, he is "rewarded" with a smack and verbal chastisement. Or maybe the owner has to chase him down and catch him in order to inflict the punishment. Guess what happens? In the first case, the dog now associates the punishment with coming when called; the owner just applied negative reinforcement to a desirable behavior, decreasing the chance that the dog will repeat it. In the second case, the dog has not a clue why he has just been assaulted, and is unlikely to continue to trust his owner, in general choosing to avoid his company in the future. So before you consider using punishment as a means of attempting behavior modification, ask

yourself if it is safe and likely to be effective, and afterwards, consider whether it actually succeeded in reducing or eliminating the target behavior.

How you choose to approach Bailey's training will be highly dependent upon the type of relationship you hope to share with your Beagle companion. Through positive reinforcement coupled with selective discipline, you can develop a mutually satisfying bond with a Beagle that will respect you and enjoy your company. Or you might attempt to use punishment as a means to force your hound into submission, with the risk that Bailey may never learn to trust you and will respond to your commands only out of fear of retribution.

Training Methods

The variety of training methods available today are numerous; no single method is perfect or likely to work effectively with every dog and in every circumstance. So how should you choose the best method for training Bailey? By taking into consideration your own personality, your Beagle's personality, your goals relating to the type of relationship you wish to have with him, and your expectations regarding more advanced training and activities. Also consider your individual abilities and experience as a trainer. Once you have decided on a method that works effectively for you and Bailey, disregard the criticisms of other dog owners who might favor a different method. But don't automatically reject suggestions for overcoming a specific training problem just because it is not in keeping with the method you are using; in a given circumstance you may find that a different approach is just what you need.

Types of Training

The instruction you will provide Bailey can be broken down into three basic types of training. Each successive level of training will begin with and build upon the basic behaviors learned during the previous type.

1. The first and most important is *manners training.* This includes all of the things you have already been doing in order to help Bailey to become a well-behaved member of the family. Manners training includes house-training, walking politely on leash, and appropriate behavior both in the home and in public.

2. Next is *obedience training,* which involves teaching Bailey to perform specific tasks on command. Traditional obedience exercises include *heeling, recall,* and *sit-stays.* While there are many benefits to formal obedience, this training is not typically aimed at improving your Beagle's behavior. The emphasis is on a precise and immediate performance in response to a command.

3. Finally, there is *activity training,* referring to advanced training for specialized activities, such as hunting, field trial competition, or Agility. This sort of training showcases Bailey's ability to perform the work for which the breed was developed or other sporting type activities that you and your Beagle might enjoy participating in together.

Agility is a form of activity training.

Food as a Tool

One of the more controversial methods of training dogs involves the use of food; yet, when used correctly, this is one of the most effective methods of training a Beagle. So why all the dissension? Some people feel that a dog should do anything you command simply because you ask it of him, and not in hopes of any reward; they expect a consistent performance based on respect and submission to the master. Others advocate the use of food in training. These trainers realize that for any dog to put forth his best effort, a reward or motivator is required. With few exceptions, food serves as the best reward and provides strong motivation for your Beagle to modify his behavior.

Unfortunately, much of the controversy is based on philosophy more so than whether or not food can be used effectively to motivate the desired performance. But there are valid points to be considered on each side. When food is repeatedly used as a *bribe*, Bailey may end up refusing to respond to your command whenever the bribe is not presented first. One must remember, however, that there is a difference between using food as a *bribe* and a *reward*.

A bribe. A bribe is an offer made in an attempt to coax the dog into doing something that it might prefer not to do. It is offered in advance in an attempt to elicit the desired behavior.

A reward. A reward is presented *after* the appropriate behavior, as a means of positive reinforcement.

Bribes should be used sparingly, and almost never as a training tool. In the setting of a potentially dangerous situation, however, bribes can be quite useful. Suppose Bailey accidentally slipped out of the door and is headed toward a busy street; if he has not yet mastered a reliable *recall*, the offer of a tasty morsel just might be the most effective means to coax him back to immediate safety.

Advocates of the food method consider bribing during training an inappropriate usage of food, instead adhering to the practice of variable reinforcement we spoke of earlier. While your hound is learning a new behavior, the rewards are more consistent, but once the behavior is understood, the food reward is presented less frequently. The result is a highly motivated Beagle that will try harder and harder to perform the appropriate action for that intermittent reward. As a trainer you will need to observe and understand your pet in order to determine the best form of motivation—food or otherwise—and the timing and frequency necessary to apply that reward effectively.

Clicker Training

A currently popular variation on the positive reinforcement method is *clicker training*. The clicker is a small plastic box with a metal strip that makes a sharp clicking sound when pushed and released. This training method makes use of a well-timed marker signal (the click sound) to communicate to the dog exactly when he is performing a desirable behavior. The click is closely followed by a food treat, praise, or whatever best serves as a reward for your Beagle. A click always means "You're doing exactly what I want" and "You're going to be rewarded."

Some people prefer the clicker method to simple reinforcement training because it is easier to master the timing of clicking during the desired behaviors. It does, however, require that you either carry a plastic clicker throughout early training or learn to substitute a vocal clicking sound. Once the dog learns the desired behavior, it's not necessary to click every occurrence, but instead, you will again be using variable reinforcement.

Direct Training

As in any approach to dog training, the objective of direct training is to help Bailey understand which are appropriate behaviors, and which actions are unacceptable. Rather than achieving this through positive, external motivation, however, your hound is given a choice to either perform as requested and receive praise or to disobey and receive an aversive consequence. The aversive consequence might be something as simple as a quick jerk and release of the leash during *heeling*. The goal is to provide perfectly timed corrections that are just unpleasant enough for the Beagle to want to avoid them.

With direct training, you would be teaching Bailey that there is a cause-and-effect relationship between his behaviors and the immediate consequences. Corrections are administered in such a way that the Beagle associates the discomfort not with you, his trainer, but with his own actions. When done correctly, direct train-

ing can more immediately curb an undesirable behavior than when we merely redirect the hound to perform an acceptable substitute action. Sounds good so far, doesn't it?

But the biggest drawback to direct training for many owners is in handling the corrections properly. In order to effectively communicate exactly what the undesired behavior was, the trainer needs to use excellent timing and expert judgment of how much force is required in administering the correction. Unfortunately, many of us have lousy timing and no clue as to how much force is too much force. Repeated, ineffective corrections may result in Bailey simply ignoring you; slip from corrections into actual punishment, and you may have just destroyed the bond you worked so hard to establish.

A Balanced Approach

In the following chapters, we will be exploring a more balanced approach to training your Beagle. While most of the methods presented will focus primarily on the use of positive reinforcement to motivate him, there are other times when the intelligent use of corrections is incorporated to enforce acceptable behavior.

Successful training of your Beagle is going to require lots of consistency, proper timing, and patience. Don't expect overnight success. Establish a training routine that includes regular, daily periods of instruction, and stick with it. In the end, he will be a much more pleasant family companion for all of your efforts.

5 The Basic Equipment

Browse through the pages of almost any pet supply catalog or web site today, and you are likely to be overwhelmed by the variety of training equipment and toys available. How does one begin to select the best possible items for the care and training of a Beagle? In reality, the basic equipment you will need for Bailey is relatively simple.

- You should have at least one collar and leash for normal, daily use, and a second set reserved for training sessions.
- A good-quality crate is one of your most essential investments, and will serve as both a secure den at home and a safe place for your Beagle to ride in during travel.
- A soft bristle brush or hound glove, toenail clippers, and doggy shampoo will suffice for routine grooming of the family companion Beagle.
- Of course you will want to provide Bailey with a number of appropriate chew items and toys in order to keep him mentally stimulated and physically active.
- Any additional training and grooming equipment required will depend specifically on whether or not you intend to participate in more advanced

activities with your Beagle, such as conformation shows, Obedience, Agility, or field work.

Collars and Leashes

A collar and leash will be among the very first items you purchase for your Beagle. He should wear a flat nylon or leather collar, complete with identification tag, for daily use. The nylon collars come in a variety of colors and fashion prints, and with either the traditional buckle or the newer, plastic quick-release closure. Adjustable nylon collars are an excellent choice for your Beagle puppy, as the size of the collar can be gradually increased as he grows. This ensures a proper fit while eliminating the need to repeatedly buy larger replacement collars for him.

Measuring Your Beagle for a Collar

To determine the appropriate size collar for your Beagle, simply measure his neck using a piece of ribbon or string. Wrap this around his neck, allowing sufficient room for you to comfortably place two fingers flat against his neck under the string. You can then mark the necessary length of string and lay it out against a ruler to determine the proper size collar to purchase. If you are buying a buckle-style collar, take the string along with you into the store to be doubly sure that you purchase the correct size. The distance from the buckle end of the collar to the center hole should be equal to the distance around your Beagle's neck. Please remember to check his collar periodically to ensure that it is not becoming too tight. As he grows, you should continue to be able to slip one or two fingers easily between his collar and neck. This will allow for a sufficiently comfortable fit without undue risk of your Beagle slipping out of his collar.

Identification

Bailey's collar not only provides you with a means for controlling him, but also is used for identification. You can easily

Crates provide safe confinement. (See page 45.)

attach an ID tag to your hound's collar that contains a name, address, and phone number for contact in case he ever becomes lost. An engraved brass tag that can be secured directly onto the collar, lying flat, is preferable to one that dangles from an "S" hook. The latter can become snagged on crates, fencing, or other items, and could result in a choking incident. Collar tags provide immediately recognizable contact information that can be used by well-meaning people to reunite a lost dog with his owners, but as a means of foolproof, permanent identification, they fall far short. There are currently three accepted methods of positive identification:

1. Tattooing your Beagle with a unique, alphanumeric identification code is the most common means of permanent identification. Typically, the dog is tattooed on the inner thigh with either a lifetime license number or registration number of some sort. One advantage of tattooing is that the identification is clearly visible to the naked eye. Tattooing is also relatively painless, and takes only a few minutes to complete. The primary drawback is that tattoos can be altered.

2. Microchip implants are rapidly gaining acceptance as a useful form of positive identification. A small chip, the approximate size of a grain of rice, is injected into the muscle mass in the area near your hound's shoulder blades. Each chip is factory-coded with a unique number that is then registered in the name of the owner. Microchips require a special scanner to read, but are a safe, permanent, and unalterable

means of identification. Most shelters and a growing number of veterinary clinics and law enforcement organizations have scanners that can be used to screen dogs for microchip implants.

3. DNA profiles are the most accurate means of identifying an individual Beagle and can be used to verify parentage as well. It is currently quite easy to acquire a test kit, swab Bailey's cheek, and then mail the sample to the AKC to be processed. For a small fee, your hound's unique DNA profile then becomes a part of his permanent AKC records.

Training Collars

Bailey's second collar and leash set should differ somewhat from his everyday equipment, and should be used strictly for training purposes. This helps your Beagle to differentiate between fun time and the time when you expect him to pay attention and act in a specific manner. During early manners training, while he is still a young puppy, you may prefer to simply snap a leash onto his flat collar. The second collar can be introduced when he is a bit more mature and ready for serious obedience work. Training collars come in a number of different styles, each designed to provide an effective means of correcting and controlling your Beagle.

Slip collars. These are a popular choice for training, but should be used with care and common sense. Sometimes referred to as a *choke chain*, the slip collar will choke Bailey only if it is used incorrectly. Slip collars come in a variety of chain

Important Tip: Never leave training equipment of any kind on your Beagle when he is not under your close supervision! As a safety precaution, always remove his training collar immediately when you are finished training and before placing him into his crate.

styles and weights, and assorted colors of braided nylon cord. To properly position the slip collar on your Beagle, hold one end in your hand and drop the chain or cord through the ring to form a loop. With Bailey facing toward you, hold the collar so that it looks like the letter P, and place it over his head. When he is in the correct heel position on your left side, the collar should pass across the top of his neck and attach to the leash, with the sliding ring hanging behind his right ear. During training, the slip collar can be used effectively to gain your Beagle's attention by giving a swift correction followed by immediate release. Practice a quick pop of the collar while it is wrapped around your own wrist first so that you will know how it feels and the proper amount of pressure to apply. Never use a slip collar to drag your Beagle around by the neck, as the constant applied force will choke him and may cause him to become frantic.

Martingales. Also called *French* or *humane choke collars*, they are an excellent choice for training or when exhibiting your Beagle at conformation shows. The double-loop construction of the martingale collar is designed so that it does

Shown is the correct position for a slip collar.

not close completely, providing even pressure around the hound's neck. If he decides to sniff the ground during training, the martingale allows you to make an instant correction and release without concern that you might apply too much pressure. Also, because the ring that attaches to the leash rides on top of the neck, corrections are applied in an upward motion. With traditional slip collars, corrections result in a sideways motion that can throw Bailey off balance and disrupt his gait in the show ring.

Prong collars. These provide another option for training. While they may look menacing, these chain collars with rows of metal prongs facing in toward the hound's neck are actually quite humane. The prongs are blunt and apply gentle pressure only in the actual direction the Beagle is pulling. If he is one of those hounds that just can't resist following his nose, dragging you around when you're out for a walk, consider trying a prong collar. You

may find it provides just enough remote correction to solve the problem, as your Beagle quickly learns that not pulling forward will release the pressure.

Halters and harnesses. Sometimes used as alternatives to a neck collar, the head halter is similar to that used on horses and other livestock, but is rarely recommended for Beagles. The theory behind halters is that where the head goes, the body follows. Body harnesses provide more gentle restraint than a collar, and eliminate tension on the neck. Harnesses are an excellent choice for exercising any Beagle that has previously suffered a ruptured disk and requires more careful handling, but because harnesses tend to encourage pulling, they are limited in their usefulness as a training aid.

Leashes

Slip leashes are especially useful for young puppies and help to prevent them from backing out of their collar and escaping. These lightweight nylon leashes have a ring on one end through which the leash passes, operating like a slip collar and leash combination all in one piece. But as Bailey grows you will soon need to begin using a sturdy snap leash attached to either his regular, flat collar or a training collar. The leash that you use during walks and basic obedience training can be almost anything that you feel comfortable with. The snap leashes of either 4 feet or 6 feet (1.2 or 1.8 m) length, made of flat nylon, cotton web, or leather are the types most commonly used for obedience training. Avoid chain leashes, as they can cause unnecessary injury to your Beagle if he becomes entangled.

Flexi leash. This is a retractable long line used for a variety of casual and training activities, including teaching your hound to come when called from a distance. Flexis allow Bailey a greater feeling of freedom, but also provide you with less control since there is no easy way to reel him in. You must use retractable leads responsibly, and only when exercising or training your Beagle in wide open spaces. Never use a Flexi near traffic or at a crowded show site, where it is advisable to keep your hound under better control for both his own safety and that of others.

Essential Supplies

- A quality crate is an excellent investment. If you own a male Beagle, or expect to do much traveling, you will probably find that the plastic

airline-style crates are the best choice. These have the advantages of being lightweight and easy to keep clean. The more open, epoxy-coated wire crates with a removable tray may be nice for female hounds, but are ineffective as a housebreaking aid for males. Once your boy starts lifting his leg, he may find it convenient to simply urinate out through the wires. Metal crates can also be especially heavy and awkward for travel use. Whichever style you choose, the intermediate size, measuring 32 inches long × 22 inches high × 23 inches wide (81 × 56 × 58 cm), is recommended for everyday use. These dimensions will allow for the average adult Beagle to stand, turn, and lie down comfortably. The medium-size crate, measuring 27 inches long × 20 inches high × 19 inches wide (68 × 51 × 48 cm), is ideal for travel, fitting nicely into the backseat of most cars.

- You will need to provide your Beagle with a pair of durable, chew-proof bowls—one each for his food and water. Stainless steel bowls are an excellent choice for both food and water, and their light weight makes them easy to clean and ideal for travel use. Special "hound bowls," with sloping sides, will prevent your Beagle's ears from becoming soiled and only rarely tip over. The 1-quart-capacity bowls are an adequate size for Beagles. Ceramic bowls are wonderful for home use, especially for water, and will not tip or spill as easily as steel bowls.

- Bedding should be comfortable and easy to clean. The beanbag-style beds are especially attractive to Beagles since they provide both comfort and security. This form of bedding usually has a removable fleece cover that is machine-washable. Imitation fleece crate pads or inexpensive bath towels serve as comfortable bedding materials for inside Bailey's crate. Avoid purchasing dog beds that are difficult to clean or have only a thin fabric cover. Beagle bedding needs to be durable or your hound is likely to entertain himself by shredding and unstuffing it!

Grooming Supplies

Routine grooming of the family companion Beagle involves little more than regular brushing of the coat to remove loose hair and dander. A hound glove or soft bristle brush are appropriate grooming tools for the Beagle's smooth-lying, medium-length coat. Ears should be inspected at weekly intervals, and can be gently cleaned using a cotton ball or cotton swab dipped in hydrogen peroxide. Toenails will also require attention. Any excess length should be trimmed back fairly close to the quick every one to two weeks. Nail clippers come in a pliers or guillotine style; whichever you choose, make sure your clipper has a good sharp blade. Styptic powder should be kept on hand to control bleeding on those occasions when you accidentally cut into the quick while trimming Bailey's nails.

Many new owners are pleasantly surprised to learn that their house Beagle will probably require a bath only once or twice a year. Realistically, he need only be bathed when he becomes especially dirty or has found something odiferous to roll in. More frequent bathing can dry out the coat and cause flaky skin. A gentle, tearless puppy shampoo may be the best type to start out with. The no-rinse, waterless shampoos are an excellent choice for the hound that requires more frequent grooming. Unless you intend to exhibit your Beagle at conformation shows, there is little need for further grooming equipment.

Toys and Treats

The best toys for your Beagle are those that appeal to his natural urges. Hounds love to chew. They also enjoy activities that satisfy their inclination to chase. Select only well-made toys for Bailey, and avoid items that might be easily torn

Brushing promotes a clean and healthy coat.

apart or inappropriately ingested. Likewise, edible treats should be selected thoughtfully. Treats should be reserved for use as rewards during training or to provide entertainment for him during his time alone. Beagles are intelligent, inquisitive canine characters. They need physical challenges and mental stimulation in their daily lives. An exuberant Beagle, left with too much spare time and not enough to do, is trouble waiting to happen. It is up to you to provide acceptable outlets for his energies.

Toys and treats can be divided into two basic categories: *interactive* and *pacifiers*. Interactive toys are those that you and Bailey can enjoy together. These include tennis balls, frisbees, and other retrievable items such as fleece or plush toys. Objects that are attractive enough to serve as motivation and rewards during training (food treats, squeaky toys, etc.) would also fall within this category. In general, most interactive toys should be picked up and put away when you are finished playing with your Beagle.

Pacifiers are toys intended to relieve boredom. Providing Bailey with chews and other safe items will help to keep him entertained when he is home alone or confined to his crate. The following toys and treats are appropriate for a Beagle and typically require little or no supervision:

■ *Nylabone, Gumabone,* and *Nylafloss* products are excellent, safe outlets for your hound's desire to chew. These nylon molded bones are flavored with real meat juices and designed to wear down slowly. They come in a variety of shapes, sizes, and hardnesses, from the edible varieties that are intended to be

Feet require special attention.

eaten, to the bones and knots designed to massage gums and clean teeth. If Bailey does not show immediate interest in these objects, try roughing up the edges and then rub peanut butter into the crevices to entice him to begin chewing

■ Edible chews are especially appealing to Beagles. Bailey is sure to enjoy such items as smoked cow or lamb ears and cow hooves. Heavy, knotted, or pressed rawhide chews will also keep your hound entertained for hours; however, rawhide products must be used with caution, as some dogs will attempt to break off and swallow large pieces. This could cause your Beagle to choke or experience digestive problems. Choose Bailey's pacifiers carefully, paying attention to selecting the right size and hardness for your hound's particular chewing style. Real bones might be safe for some Beagles, but should be avoided if you intend to show Bailey, as heavy chewers can suffer from tooth fractures. Never offer your hound chicken bones or other types of bone that could splinter or break apart and be ingested. You may also want to exercise caution regarding pig ears and related items; these can cause digestive upsets due to the excessive amounts of grease. Care must be used when handling, due to the potential for salmonella bacteria exposure.

- Knotted ropes made from braided cotton strands serve to massage gums and help prevent plaque buildup. Beagles also enjoy shaking, tossing, pouncing upon, and "killing" their rope toys as an expression of prey instinct. Some ropes have rubber chew toys or tennis balls attached to them for even more fun. You can use a knotted rope either as a safe pacifier or as an interactive toy during a game of Fetch.

- Dental devices come in a variety of shapes and sizes and feature either raised nubs or dental floss. Some are even designed so that you can apply doggy toothpaste to help keep your Beagle's teeth clean and breath fresh.

- *Buster cubes* are a favorite toy for providing your Beagle with both physical exercise and a mental challenge. These durable plastic cubes randomly dispense small treats as he rolls the cube across the floor with his nose or paws. The Buster cube will provide your hound with an excellent workout and requires only minimal involvement on your part. If you find that he is overly enthusiastic in his approach to emptying the cube, you may need to supervise or restrict cube play to outdoors.

- *Kongs* are tough rubber toys that look like rattlesnake tails and bounce in random directions when thrown. They are hollow so that you can stuff them with doggy treats or peanut butter. *Planet* pet toys are similar, but shaped like balls or spaceships with gripping holes that are perfect for holding smaller treats. Fill several and then hide them around the house or yard. Your Beagle will be entertained for hours.

- For outdoor play, Bailey might enjoy splashing in a child's wading pool on warm summer days. Toss a few ice cubes into the water and watch him bob for them. If your Beagle is a confirmed digger, provide him with his own personal sandbox in a shady corner of the yard. Bury a few favorite chew toys or treats in the sand on occasion for your hound to discover.

6 House-training and Basic Manners

Your Ideal Companion

Like most owners, you probably wanted a dog primarily for the companionship dogs provide. When you selected a Beagle in particular, it was because you felt the breed was well suited to your lifestyle and in keeping with your expectations. But no matter how intelligent and affectionate your Beagle is, he is not going to become your ideal canine companion without some basic training.

You want Bailey to learn to be clean in the house, to come to you when called, walk politely on a leash, and in general to behave in a socially appropriate manner, both at home and in public. Through basic training you will begin to shape your Beagle's behaviors while at the same time laying the foundation for the possibility of future participation together in more advanced activities. The first and most important lesson he must learn if he is to become a welcome family member is his house-training.

House-training

All dogs should be housebroken and crate-trained, regardless of whether or not they are eventually going to be housed outdoors or will spend their entire lives indoors as family companions. Why should you house-train Bailey, even if he is going to be a hunting dog that resides in an outdoor kennel? The advantages to doing so are numerous. Bringing your new Beagle into the home, even temporarily, gives you a much better opportunity to form a strong bond with him. Doing so also aids in establishing yourself as his pack leader. Even the hunting Beagle needs to learn basic manners and to respond to the master's commands. When you do eventually take your Beagle afield, it will be a safer and more satisfying experience if he hunts *with* you and *for* you, respectfully obeying your directions. There are also going to be those times in any hound's life when it becomes necessary to bring him indoors and/or confine him to the crate. These include when he is recuperating from illness or injury, during severe weather conditions, or when traveling. A crate-trained, housebroken Beagle will be much more pleasant to deal with during these times.

Crate Training

As mentioned earlier, one of the best investments you will ever make for your Beagle's welfare is the purchase of a good-quality crate. Place the crate in a high-use room, and use it wisely to provide a secure den for your hound whenever you must leave him unattended for short periods of time. As long as it is not abused, the crate will become his special place, a secure den of his own, excellent sleeping quarters, and a safe place to ride in when traveling.

1. Start using the crate from the very first day you bring Bailey into your home. When initially introducing him to his

Basic training lays the foundation for future achievements.

crate, place it in a commonly used area such as the kitchen or family room. Toss a few favorite toys and some tasty treats into the open crate and allow the hound to come and go as he pleases.

2. At mealtimes, always feed Bailey in his crate and with the door closed. When he has finished eating, release him and allow him to get a drink of fresh water, then take him outside immediately to eliminate. Through associative learning, Bailey should soon come to view his crate as a pleasant place to be, his own private den.

3. Use the crate as a safe place to confine Bailey when you cannot watch him every second. While the family has dinner, put him in his crate. When the phone rings or someone comes to your door, crate him before you answer. While you are away at work during the day or out running errands, your hound can wait safely in his crate.

4. Whenever you need a break from puppy watching, crate him. He should eat, nap, and sleep in his crate. Ignore any fussing or protest, and avoid speaking to him while he is crated. Never release him from the crate when he is making a fuss. If he learns that creating a noisy commotion gains your attention and gets him out of the crate, he will protest even louder the next time.

5. When Bailey is obviously tired and ready for a nap, place him in his crate. As soon as you hear him start to wake up, go to him, pick him up, and carry him outside. Always try to reach the crate promptly, before Bailey launches

into a fit of barking or howling; you don't want to inadvertently reward him for being noisy.

6. He should also learn to sleep in his crate at night. When he wakes during the night, go to him and take him out for a potty break. Pick him up and carry him outdoors to prevent an accident in the house. You want him to develop confidence that you will meet his bathroom needs, but this is not playtime, and nighttime potty trips should remain all business. As soon as he has relieved himself, you should return him to the crate to sleep the remainder of the night.

There are several important rules to remember when crate training.

■ Select a size crate with dimensions large enough to allow your Beagle to stand up, turn around, and lie down comfortably.

■ Always remove all collars and leashes when placing him in the crate, as they could present a choking hazard. The one exception is while traveling, at which time it may be advisable to keep a flat collar with identification on him at all times.

■ Provide safe chew items only for your Beagle's entertainment while confined to the crate. These might include chew hooves, smoked cow ears, or a Nylabone.

■ Children should know that the crate is your Beagle's *private room*; they should never disturb him while he is crated, or play in the crate when he is not in it.

■ Like any form of confinement, crate time must be balanced with sufficient exercise and human companionship. Excessive periods of isolation can contribute to a variety of undesirable behav-

iors including frenzied or destructive behavior, self-mutilation, and inappropriate barking.

■ And finally, never, *ever*, use confinement to the crate as a means of punishment.

When the crate is utilized correctly, most dogs enjoy and use them regularly. The crate provides a secure, quiet place where Bailey can go to escape household goings-on and to rest peacefully. It is also the safest place to leave your new Beagle when he cannot be carefully supervised. The majority of dogs naturally prefer to keep their den area clean and will try not to urinate or defecate in the crate. This is why the crate can be so invaluable as a housebreaking aid.

The Crate as a Housebreaking Aid

A commonly asked question is "Are Beagles difficult to house-train?" In truth, no more so than any dog, although there will be normal variation among individuals regarding how long it will take to reliably house-train. The key elements to successful housebreaking are timing, consistency, confinement, and positive reinforcement. The most efficient method in the majority of cases is to confine your Beagle to his crate when you cannot closely supervise his actions. The theory behind the crate-training method is that dogs instinctively dislike soiling their "den," and will attempt to wait until released to the appropriate outdoor location to relieve themselves. To be effective, the crate should be just large enough for Bailey to turn around and lie down in; if the area is

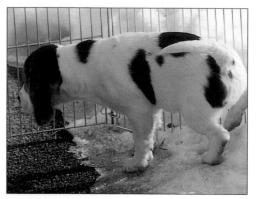

Good puppy!

Special tip: During the house-training process, it is advisable to physically pick up your Beagle puppy and carry him outdoors when he first wakes from a nap in his crate; otherwise, he is likely to take a few steps out of the crate and then urinate on the floor.

too large, he may find it acceptable to eliminate at one end of his crate and then sleep comfortably at the other end.

Be very consistent right from the start. Always crate Bailey when you cannot properly supervise him and then immediately take him outside to eliminate when you release him from the crate. To properly house-train your pet, it is important not to give him the opportunity to repeatedly have accidents; such behavior is likely to become a very difficult habit to break. Never allow him freedom to roam the home unsupervised before he is very reliably housebroken—this is where many

people make their biggest mistake. You must be consistent, even if your Beagle buddy protests the restricted activities.

Never rely on a young puppy to tell you when he needs to eliminate. It is your responsibility as the trainer to understand when he needs to go outside. Observe his activity level, keep an eye out for warning behaviors, and watch the clock. A three-month-old puppy that is active and playing may need to urinate as frequently as every 15 to 20 minutes, or sooner. Physical activity produces urine; inactivity slows the production. A resting puppy might hold his urine for an hour or more. And while it typically will take at least a few weeks to develop good control, the sleeping puppy soon learns to hold his urine overnight.

A schedule. It is important to develop and maintain a proper schedule with your Beagle. Take him out first thing in the morning, after each meal, each nap, and last thing before you retire at night. Over the first few weeks expect to get up at least once during the night to provide a potty break, especially if Bailey is still a young puppy when he comes into your home. Teaching nighttime bladder control will progress more quickly if you carefully structure your puppy's evening routine. Play vigorously with him in order to wear him out, then take him to the designated area to eliminate. Don't give him any food, water, or treats after about 8:30 P.M.

Supervise. Supervise closely when Bailey is playing or exploring in the house.
1. Watch for telltale signals that he may be preparing to eliminate, such as sniff-

ing in circles, frantic pacing back and forth and whining, or sudden loss of interest in play and heading for a remote location. When this happens, immediately take him outside to the desired location. Tell him where you are going, using a command such as *"Outside!"* and go directly to the designated potty area. Try to keep him focused on the reason you are out there. Do not go for a walk, play, or give him any special attention until after he has done his business.

2. As soon as Bailey does begin to relieve himself, reward with plenty of praise. Use verbal praise *during* the act to reinforce elimination, but reserve petting, treats, and play as rewards for afterwards. You want him to know that you are very pleased with his having relieved himself in the designated area, but you don't want to distract him from completing his business.
3. Always take a few moments to be sure that Bailey has finished before you head back indoors; puppies will often urinate a second time within a period of several minutes.

Soon, Bailey will learn that the word *"Outside"* is associated with elimination, followed by a reward. Eventually you should be able to ask him "Do you have to go *outside*?" and elicit a response such as barking or running to the door.

Accidents. As for the occasional spotting around the house: accidents will happen, especially when Bailey is not closely supervised. Remember that young puppies often need to relieve themselves quite frequently. Ignore mistakes and

praise/reward all successes. If your Beagle makes a mistake it is because you didn't take him out when you should have—it's not his fault! Also avoid the temptation to punish him for accidents that occur while you are away from home. He is unlikely to associate your displeasure with his having eliminated several hours earlier, and you will only confuse him. Be sure to clean up all accidents extremely well, or Bailey is likely to return to the scene of the crime later and *mark* the same spot. We recommend that you purchase and use one of the enzymatic cleaners that remove all traces of odor; avoid ammonia-based products.

Another common mistake made by new owners is to confine a puppy for lengths of time that exceed his ability to hold his urine. This forces the puppy to use the crate as a potty, and quickly negates its effectiveness as a housebreaking aid. Remember that the crate must be used wisely, and that Bailey must learn to develop control. Initially he might not be physically able to hold his urine for more than a few hours at a time, but with patience and consistency on your part, he will eventually develop bladder control, establish a routine for voiding, and learn the appropriate location to do so.

Paper Training

Another common method of housebreaking involves the intermediate step of teaching your hound to eliminate on papers or specially treated pads. If you prefer not to risk exposing your new Beagle to other dogs until after he has completed all of his booster vaccinations, paper training may be an acceptable option.

1. Whenever you see Bailey beginning his prepotty rituals, sniffing around or turning circles, gently pick him up and place him on the papers to do his business.

2. As he begins to eliminate, tell him repeatedly *"Potty, potty"* or whatever term you prefer, and then praise him. Assigning a word to his elimination will help to ease the transition when you begin to teach him to eliminate outdoors.

3. Eventually, through repetition and positive reinforcement, your Beagle will become reliable about using the papered area for elimination, even when unsupervised. Over time, you can begin to move his papers to a location closer to the door, ultimately doing away with the papers altogether and encouraging Bailey to do his business outside. One of the disadvantages to this method is that, for a time at least, you are actually encouraging your Beagle to eliminate inside the home. Paper training also tends to prolong the housebreaking period.

Housebreaking the Adult

If Bailey is already an adult, he may have received some prior house-training. Regardless of whether or not he might have been housebroken in a previous home, it is always wise to begin your relationship by reinforcing house manners and treating him as you would any untrained puppy. Keep in mind that Bailey probably finds all of these changes and new experiences quite stressful. He must make a multitude of adjustments, learn where he is to sleep, and determine which doors lead to outside. Beagles are adaptable characters, but even these little guys can find such major changes a bit unsettling.

One of the most important things you should do upon arriving home is to introduce Bailey to his new yard or exercise area. Allow him to explore for a few minutes, and then encourage him to eliminate before entering the house. When he does finally do his business, be certain to praise him and let him know in no uncertain terms that he has performed an appropriate behavior and you are pleased. Because he is no longer a young puppy, Bailey should have better-developed bowel and bladder control. Yet, just as with a puppy, you need to establish a regular schedule for elimination. Take him outside at specific times, whether he asks to go out or not. The more rapidly outdoor elimination is established as a habit, the sooner Bailey can become a trusted member of the household.

Health and Diet

There are a few more matters to take into consideration during house-breaking. Your Beagle's current state of health will affect his ability to be successfully house-trained. As was mentioned earlier, Bailey should be examined by a veterinarian within the first few days of coming into your home. It is important that any physical conditions that could impede successful house-training, such as cystitis, bladder infections, etc., be diagnosed and properly treated. Examination of a stool sample will identify any intestinal parasites if present. Sudden changes in water and diet can lead to bouts of diarrhea, which also make controlled elimination difficult for the dog. Avoid feeding table scraps or canned, moist dog foods. Stick to a high-quality brand of dry kibble. If you should choose to change Bailey's diet for any reason, do it gradually over a period of four to seven days—by overlapping both the old and the new brands of kibble together, until the old food has been completely phased out.

Teaching the Basics

Before we begin teaching Bailey the basic commands, let's review a few of the *rules* one more time:

1. Always be consistent; choose one command word for each desired behavior and use that word consistently during training.
2. Keep training sessions short and pleasant.
3. Use positive reinforcement through well-timed praise and rewards.
4. Make sure the reward is sufficient to motivate Bailey to want to repeat the behavior again.
5. Discipline when necessary, using the mildest correction that you find effective.
6. Do not repeatedly use a correction that does not work—and never give a command to your Beagle during training that you cannot enforce.

Taming Hyperactivity

Settle! There will be those moments in Bailey's life when he is just too full of himself, especially during adolescence. When you need to calm down your exuberant Beagle buddy and refocus his attention, *"Settle!"* and *"Watch me!"* are two commands that can help. Suppose you are attending your first puppy training class, and Bailey is so excited at the prospect of all these new friends to play with that he has seemingly forgotten all manners. You've tried the *sit* command, but he doesn't even seem to hear you; his mind is definitely elsewhere. How do you get him to calm down and start thinking rather than acting? Give the command *"Settle!"* in an authoritative voice, while reaching down and giving him a firm but gentle *nose hug* (see page 30) with one hand and placing the other hand squarely on his shoulders. This mirrors the canine behavior pretty effectively, and usually works quite well at calming the hyperactive Beagle.

A gentle nose hug calms hyperactivity.

Home Schooling

Sit

The very first simple command you should teach Bailey is *"Sit."* The *sit* is the foundation for all other obedience exercises. You will find that the *sit* is very useful, particularly when you need to calm your Beagle and focus his attention back on you.

Begin by putting on Bailey's training collar and attaching his leash (see chapter 5). Take him to a quiet location, free from distractions. With your Beagle positioned beside you on your left side, give the command *Bailey, sit!* At the same time, push down firmly on his hindquarters with your left hand while pulling the leash straight up with your

Use your hands to ease your Beagle into the *sit*.

right hand. As soon as he complies by sitting, verbally praise him to reinforce the behavior. Try to have him hold the position for at least a few seconds, being prepared to use your hands to place him back into position if he breaks too soon. When he has remained sitting politely for a few moments, give the release command *Okay!* and reward him with a tasty treat. Beagles typically master the *sit* very quickly, and soon you can begin to practice longer *sits* and incorporate the *sit* into other areas of training. As with all desirable behaviors, if you see Bailey sitting on his own, take advantage of the opportunity to identify and further reinforce the behavior.

What are some of the situations where you can use *"Sit"* to better control Bailey's behavior? Many trainers take the approach of teaching a dog that nothing in life is free. In order to earn his dinner or a treat, Bailey must show his respect for you by obeying the *sit* command first. Suppose it is time for your Beagle's walk, and he is bouncing off the walls in excitement? Have him sit so that you can put on his collar and leash. Do not wrestle with an overexuberant hound while attempting to put on his collar. Bailey should learn that he must *sit* before you will reward him by taking him anywhere. Likewise, teaching him to always sit before he is permitted to go through the doorway may in turn prevent his making a mad dash for freedom every time someone opens a door.

Walking Politely On Leash

"Walkies!" or *"Walk"* is the command used when you want to take Bailey for a pleasant walk around the neighborhood. This is not the same as the *heel* command, which should be reserved for the formal obedience exercise involving a much greater level of concentration and precision. During the actual *heel,* which can be taught later, Bailey is required to walk on your left side, in a position even with your knee, and must sit every time you stop.

To introduce Bailey to his collar and leash, start by snapping them on during a supervised play session in the house. Allow him to drag the leash behind him as he romps about, but discourage him from chewing on it. Most puppies will initially react to the feel of a collar around their neck by stopping and scratching at it frequently, but they soon learn to ignore it.

Next, you should pick up the leash and encourage Bailey to walk along with you, using the *"Walkies!"* command issued in a pleasant voice. The best way to encourage your Beagle to want to stay near you without pulling and fighting the leash is to make this exercise into a fun game. Reward him for staying close and moving in your direction by periodically offering a treat or favorite toy. Never jerk him off balance or drag him by the neck; you want him to enjoy walking with you. Keep the experience as pleasant as pos-

These dogs are taking a polite group walk.

sible, using positive reinforcement to reassure him that submitting to the leash is a good thing.

Once Bailey is comfortable with his collar and leash, take him out into the yard. Tell him *"Bailey, walkies!"* and begin to walk away at a fast pace. If he immediately follows along, stop after 10 to 15 feet (3–5 m) and praise and reward. If he is hesitant or balks, gently use the leash to reel him in, then give him a treat and vocal praise when he reaches your side. Repeat the exercise, going in a different direction this time. After a few repetitions and consistently receiving positive reinforcement (treats), Bailey should be more than happy to follow along with you on walks. After several days, add a new variation to the exercise. Instead of stopping, go a short distance and then suddenly change direction. Start running backwards in small steps, while telling him *"Walkies."* When he turns

Home Schooling

and catches up with you, praise and reward. Eventually you can begin to decrease the frequency of rewards, and should need to repeat the *walk* command only when he fails to immediately respond to your change of direction. Keeping up with you and being aware of your position becomes a fun game. Continue to praise each time he responds positively, but once he understands the concept, use treats as an intermittent reward.

The Recall

Teaching Bailey to come when called is one of the most important lessons he will ever learn. While still a young puppy, Bailey is highly dependent on you and instinctively follows you everywhere, readily coming when you call his name. Don't be fooled. As he reaches adolescence he is going to become more of an independent thinker. One day, when he is busy exploring an interesting scent, he will ignore your call. Never lie to yourself about how reliably you have trained him to come on command. If you do, it's his life you are gambling with.

How do you teach Bailey a reliable *recall*? It all starts with establishing a good relationship. Bailey should enjoy being with you and look to you as the bearer of all good things in life—food, affection, toys, and a secure environ-

ment. Until he is properly trained, never allow him off leash outdoors, unless he is in a safely fenced yard. A truly reliable *recall* may take months of consistent positive reinforcement to achieve. He should learn to love the word *"Come,"* associating it only with pleasant experiences.

■ Never use the *come* command to call Bailey to you in order to dispense discipline, bathe him, trim toenails, or anything else he might find disagreeable. Why should he willingly run to you if the *recall* is going to result in an unpleasant experience? He should learn that *come* always means something good is about to happen.

■ Until Bailey's response is reliable, never use the *come* command unless you can enforce the behavior, either by keeping him on leash or by having a second person put his or her hands on the hound to back up your command.

■ If you need Bailey for any reason, and do not have a way to enforce the *recall*, go and physically get him. Don't repeatedly test the *come* command until you are confident of his response.

■ If you want to train a reliable *recall*, never play games with Bailey in which you chase him. In fact, never chase him at all unless it is an actual emergency. Instead play games where he must chase and catch you! Be creative; get down on the floor and play bow if necessary, then crawl away. You want your Beagle to think it is fun to always chase and follow you, at the same time teaching him never to run away.

Initially, we are not going to expect Bailey to perform a perfect obedience *recall*. Teaching the formal exercise with a *sit* in front can come later. Remember, we want to keep the *recall* fun. For the earliest lessons, you may want to ask a friend or family member to assist you. Bring Bailey to a location in the house where there will be few distractions. Sit comfortably on the floor at opposite ends of the room, and then take turns calling him to you in an enthusiastic and playful tone of voice. Act silly, make odd noises, clap, do whatever necessary to encourage him to come to you. When he does so, hug him, praise him, and reward with some tasty treats. Always let him know that you are very pleased with his appropriate behavior. Carry a few treats in your pocket while at home, and whenever he is already coming to you take advantage of the situation. Use the command *"Bailey, come!"* when he is within a couple of feet of reaching you. When he arrives in front of you a few seconds later, praise him and reward with a treat.

Next you will want to move Bailey's training outdoors, where there are more distractions. Keep him on leash so that you can always enforce the command if he does not immediately respond. Call *"Bailey, come!"* and if he does not start toward you on his own, give a gentle tug on the leash to encourage him in the right direction. If necessary, use the leash to reel him all the way in to you. Praise and reward him when he does come, even if you had to make him do it. As his performance improves, you can begin to practice the *recall* from more of a distance, using a retractable leash instead of the 6-foot (1.8-m) leash (see Chapter 5). When he is coming to you every time you call, you can start working off leash in a confined area. Have a friend assist you by staying within arm's length of your Beagle in order to enforce the command should he ignore you. Allow Bailey to sniff about and explore, then give the *come* command. If he does not come consistently, then you will need to go back and further reinforce the *recall* before trusting him off leash outdoors.

A reliable *recall* requires lots of practice.

Note: If Bailey seems to have an excess of energy and difficulty concentrating during training, you may simply need to exercise him more. Take long walks, play games of Fetch, and occasionally go places where he can safely run off leash. Try to find creative outlets for all of his youthful energies. If your Beagle is mature enough, enroll in training classes and try something fun for both of you, such as Agility.

Watch me! Once you've got your Beagle's attention, how do you keep it? By teaching him the positive behavior of consistently looking to you for guidance. When you notice his mind beginning to wander during training, a quick reminder to *"Watch me"* can bring him back into focus. To teach him to focus on your face, and to look to you for direction, begin by having him sit facing you. By now he is probably aware of the pocket in which you carry treats for rewards. Place your hand in the treat pocket and quickly draw your hand out and up toward your face, at the same time commanding "Watch me!" Bailey is going to be very focused on your face. Make friendly eye contact with him for a few moments, then praise and reward. Remember, you are not making *alpha* eye contact, which is intimidating to a dog, but instead being friendly and communicative. Once he learns to respond to the command by focusing on you, begin to use verbal praise with only intermittent additional rewards.

While you are out for a walk with Bailey, occasionally get his attention by calling his name, clicking your tongue, or squeaking a toy in your pocket. When he looks up at you, repeat *"Watch me,"* then praise him for focusing his attention on you. Release him and allow him to continue with his walk. You will soon find that he is happier and more secure, and also performing better, when you help him to stay focused on you during training or competition.

Leave It!

Beagles are forever following their noses into trouble. When Bailey finds a potentially dangerous or inappropriate "prize," you can divert his attention by using the command to *"Leave it!"* Training your Beagle to respond to the *leave it* command involves setting him up a bit. Put on his collar and leash before you begin, so that you have a means of controlling his actions. Now leave within reach something you know he will find tempting, such as a plate of cookies. When you catch Bailey about to take one, physically stop him from doing so, tell him *"Leave it!"* then praise and reward with an especially tasty treat (*not* one of the cookies!). The goal is to teach your Beagle that no matter how tempting an item might be, when he passes it up and responds to your command to *"Leave it,"* he is going to get something even better. Through setups, you can also teach him what sort of items he can think about taking, and what is strictly off limits. However, Beagles will be Beagles, and if you intend to share your life and home with one of these inquisitive scenthounds there is no excuse for not taking proper precautions. Just because Bailey no longer steals cookies from the kitchen countertop while you are present does not mean he can reliably resist temptation when there is no one watching. Never expect more of your Beagle than what you know deep down he is capable of.

Games and Activities

Playing games with your Beagle can be fun, and also teaches valuable social lessons. Make sure to take time out from more formal training to engage in play with him. If he occasionally becomes overexcited or too rough during play, stop immediately. Let him calm down and then continue in a more controlled manner. Games with rules can help to reinforce your leadership position, while providing mental stimulation and exercise for your Beagle. Best of all, structured games and activities provide opportunity for you and Bailey to enjoy each other's company.

Find the Treat/Toy

This game combines two of your Beagle's favorite activities: scent work and eating! While Bailey is in another room, lay out a widely spaced trail of kibbles leading to his hidden food bowl. Then bring him in and show him the first kibble or two, telling him *"Find your treats!"* Most hounds catch on very quickly to searching for food items. Gradually decrease the

This Beagle is learning to focus on his handler.

number of clues along the trail until Bailey is searching for and finding the hidden food bowl all on his own. Once he understands the concept, try hiding a dog biscuit or favorite toy instead. If your Beagle has learned to identify specific toys by name, you can even send him off to locate and retrieve his toys one by one, using commands such as *"Find your ball."* What better way to keep your scenthound's mind busy than through searching games!

Hide-and-Seek

Encouraging your Beagle to search for and find a friendly person is a fun game that also lays the groundwork for activities such as tracking or search and rescue. One person should hold Bailey's collar while another family member leaves the room to go hide. Have the hidden person call *"Bailey, come!"* Then release your hound to go and find the missing person. Initially, you may need to help Bailey to search for him or her. When the person is located, he or she should respond to Bailey with praise and affection. Start out with easy hiding spots, and gradually make the game more challenging day by day. Eventually, you may be able to present your Beagle with an article of clothing belonging to the person and tell him to *"Go find."* Playing this game in the dark will also encourage your hound to use his nose to follow the scent trail and locate the hidden person.

Obstacle Courses

Beagles enjoy a physical challenge. You can set up a simple obstacle course using anything handy that your hound can safely climb over, under, around, or through. A child's play tunnel or old cardboard boxes can be fun obstacles for your Beagle to investigate. A landscape timber or a flat board laid on top of bricks or blocks becomes a simple bridge. Step stools or a few pieces of firewood are obstacles to be climbed over. Add a small jump or two. Just remember to start slowly and keep jumps low at first. Make sure that the landing surface is smooth and soft, and *never* force exercise on a young Beagle whose bones and joints are still developing. A home obstacle course can be a fun way to introduce Bailey to future Agility work.

Simple Tricks

The variety of tricks that you can teach your Beagle to perform will be limited only by your imagination. Many tricks are also beneficial in shaping desirable behavior patterns. Just remember to keep training fun, and provide plenty of positive motivation.

Shaking hands. This is a trick that involves teaching your Beagle to voluntarily lift his feet on command. This can be especially useful when it comes time to trim toenails, or if you need to check Bailey's feet for injury after field work. It is also a nice way to have your hound greet people, since the trick is performed in the sitting position. Begin by having Bailey sit. Command *"Shake"* and then gently take one front paw in your hand. While holding his paw, praise and reward him, and then release. Repeat several times each day. Eventually your Beagle will begin to respond to the command by lifting his paw when you say *"Shake"* without your having to show him what to do.

Take a nap, or Play dead. This is a game that gets your Beagle out from underfoot without requiring that he be confined to his crate. Take him to his dog bed or another comfortable spot and have him lie down. Gently roll him onto his side while commanding *"Nap time"* or *"Play dead."* While he remains lying down for a few moments, praise and reward, then release him, saying *"Wake up,"* and let him stand up again. Once the trick of lying down for a nap is mastered, sending him to his bed to settle down for longer periods can buy you some quiet time.

Physical Exercise

Additional forms of physical exercise that are appropriate for your Beagle include jogging and hiking with his human family. Always remember to start slowly and gradually build up to greater distances. Young hounds should be allowed to run only on soft surfaces to avoid injury to growing joints, and never pushed to continue once fatigued. Check Bailey's footpads prior to and after each run for possible injury. Retrieving is a wonderful, interactive game that provides plenty of exercise (see page 80). Swimming is also an excellent workout and fun summer activity. Not all hounds take to the water naturally, however. Introduce Bailey to the water gradually, and consider using a doggy life jacket if you take him boating with you. Even with hounds that know how to swim, pools should be strictly off limits when your pet is unsupervised.

Dog Sports

For many people, one of the most enjoyable aspects of Beagle ownership involves participating in more advanced dog sports and activities. Over 15,000 competitive canine events are held annually under American Kennel Club rules. These AKC events can be divided into three basic categories: conformation shows; obedience, tracking and Agility trials; and performance events such as the various formats of Beagle field trials. Successful competition in these events can lead to your Beagle earning titles, which then become a permanent part of his official AKC records. Whether you choose to participate in advanced dog sports as an exhibitor or prefer to remain a spectator is relatively unimportant. Attending shows and performance events is an opportunity to share in the enjoyment and

appreciation for all that our versatile canine companions can be.

Troubleshooting

Training Classes

For some reason, our society tends to embrace the belief that anyone can effectively train his or her own dog. The truth is that many of us simply lack the commitment, patience, or sense of timing required to properly train a Beagle at home without additional outside guidance. You may find it well worth your while to attend a structured obedience training class with Bailey, especially if you lack prior experience in training dogs.

The first thing to consider when selecting a class to attend is whether or not you are comfortable with the instructor and

Swimming is good exercise.

his or her methods. If you are able to observe a training class in advance, then certainly do so. Remember that if you are uncomfortable with the training methods being used, or dislike the instructor's attitude, you and Bailey are unlikely to come away with anything positive from those classes. It is also important that the class be organized in a way that enables you to learn to train and handle your own Beagle. You should be instructed how to communicate with him and conduct yourself during training, so that he will better understand the lessons you are trying to teach—so choose a training class carefully.

1. **How Do You Locate Training Classes?** If you purchased your Beagle locally, his breeder may have some suggestions. You might also access the AKC web site (see the links provided in Useful Addresses and Literature, page 143) to find contact information for those obedience or all-breed kennel clubs located within a moderate distance of your home. Most clubs will either sponsor training classes themselves or can recommend several reputable trainers within your area that do hold them. Your veterinarian will probably also know where there are training classes in your general area that you might consider attending.

2. **At What Age Can He Begin?** Even if Bailey is just a young puppy, you won't need to wait long before he can begin to attend classes. Many clubs and trainers offer what they call a *Puppy Kindergarten* class, for puppies three months of age and up, which provides very basic manners training and socialization. As soon as your Beagle has completed his series of protective vaccinations, he can begin to safely venture out in public. This early training is aimed more at bonding and laying the groundwork for future, more structured activities. Just as was suggested with your home training, be sure to keep kindergarten classes fun for your young Beagle, and have patience. Bailey is still very much a puppy. Formal obedience training typically may begin after Bailey has reached six months of age. If this is your first experience with training a Beagle, it is recommended that you enroll in at least the *beginner obedience* classes in order to master basic training techniques, such as *sit, stay, come on command.*

3. **What Are the Advantages to Attending Weekly Training Classes?** Attending obedience classes will help you to develop more effective timing for the administration of rewards and corrections during training. You also will have access to an experienced dog trainer who should be both capable and willing to answer all of your specific training questions. And perhaps most importantly, attending weekly training classes can provide that much-needed motivation to consistently work with your dog throughout the week. When home training alone, it becomes so easy to repeatedly put off your hound's lessons until tomorrow, especially after a long day at the office. But the thought of being embarrassed by your untrained Beagle at Wednesday night's class just might be inspiration enough for you to allocate those necessary five to ten minutes to his daily

instruction. You might even be pleasantly surprised to discover that both you and Bailey actually enjoy the social interaction of attending group training classes.

Canine Adolescence

Unless you acquired an adult Beagle or older puppy, Bailey probably joined your household while he was still young enough to be highly dependent on you. Initially, your puppy may have come running every time you called his name and followed you around adoringly. He even seemed to learn all of his early lessons so quickly and reliably that you began to think he must be the most perfect Beagle ever born. Then suddenly, almost overnight, your sweet little Beagle buddy has turned into a brat! He seems to have forgotten everything you ever taught him and can be downright defiant at times. You thought he was housebroken, but now he will look you straight in the eye as he hikes his leg to water the living room sofa. What happened?

Welcome to canine adolescence! Just as human teenagers go through a stage of testing their own independence, Bailey is also likely to explore his options and try your patience. He may ignore your commands just to see what your reaction will be. His raging hormones and newfound confidence may result in a plethora of behaviors that make you crazy. But take heart—if handled correctly, he will come

through this adolescent period just fine and will mature into a pleasant, adult companion animal.

Adolescence is closely related to the onset of sexual maturity, usually occurring between six and nine months of age, although some Beagles may begin to "test their wings" much earlier. Certain individual hounds will experience a second fear impact period at some point during the adolescent stage, where they exhibit seemingly irrational fears of new situations or specific objects. Try to be patient and allow Bailey to work through such fears on his own. Be careful not to inadvertently reinforce fearful behavior by attempting to reassure him with petting or praise. By 18 to 24 months of age, he will begin to settle into adulthood.

We bring up a discussion of adolescence here because it is important to understand that this is a perfectly natural stage in your Beagle's development. While adolescence may be a rather trying period in his life, it is also an exuberant one. By channeling his energy and enthusiasm into fun activities, exercise, and work, you can make his adolescence much more enjoyable for both of you. It is especially important during this time to always enforce all commands and to be especially consistent about what you expect from him. Adolescent Beagles can be particularly stubborn creatures, but through patient guidance and understanding, you can establish a satisfying relationship with your hound that will last for many years.

7 *Tackling Nuisance Behaviors*

Many of the behavioral problems of dogs are merely part of natural canine conduct that has become misdirected or occurs at an inappropriate time or place. In some cases, your Beagle's misbehavior may be rooted in a lack of respect for the human members of the household, particularly if you have failed to properly establish the rules of social hierarchy. Any time an inappropriate behavior becomes evident, it should inspire a change in the way that you are dealing with your Beagle. Without intervention, he is unlikely to *outgrow* the problem. The following is an alphabetical listing of some of the more common nuisance behaviors, offering insight into their possible causes and suggestions for dealing with them.

Common Nuisance Behaviors

Aggression

Aggression is clearly the most disturbing and potentially dangerous of all canine behavior problems. When left unchecked, an aggression problem can culminate in human injury, and ultimately in euthana-sia of the dog. Modifying the behavior of an aggressive Beagle that bites or seriously threatens to bite may well be beyond the capabilities of the average owner or group training class. If Bailey is already acting aggressively to the point that he sometimes frightens you, we highly recommend that you seek professional help. Look for an experienced trainer or behaviorist who is willing to come into your home and personally evaluate your Beagle.

In general, the vast majority of Beagles do not tend to be especially aggressive. As a *pack-oriented* hound, Bailey is far more likely to have an easygoing, friendly temperament. But there are situations in which Beagles can tend to demonstrate a certain amount of dominance-related aggression. Such behavior is more easily prevented than treated. Dominance aggression is best inhibited by firmly establishing Bailey's subordinate position within the social hierarchy of your household. Be sure to properly socialize your Beagle, practicing all of the dominance and bonding exercises recommended in Chapter 4 of this book.

When a normally gentle Beagle suddenly becomes aggressive, always consult your veterinarian first. Many times

Sharing furniture erodes your dominant status.

Your Beagle should know his position in the social hierarchy.

seemingly aggressive behavior may be the result of the dog experiencing pain or discomfort in relation to a health problem. He can't tell you he is hurting, but may growl or nip to warn you away from touching him. If your veterinarian fails to turn up any physical causes for his bad attitude, he might at least be able to provide you with contact information for an experienced trainer.

Aggression can be divided into three basic categories. These include:
1. Aggression toward owner(s)
2. Aggression toward strangers
3. Aggression toward other animals

If Bailey is acting aggressively toward family members, it could be due to a feeling of dominance, or might alternatively be fear related. The Beagle that guards his possessions or food, growls when you

attempt to remove him from your couch, or challenges your authority is acting upon his perceived social dominance. Don't attempt to physically punish or force a confrontation with this type of aggressive hound. To do so may escalate the aggression and result in personal injury. The most effective approach is to recondition Bailey to accept the dominance of his human family members through *positive reinforcement* and *behavior modification*. For the Beagle that is snapping out of fear, your efforts should be aimed at reducing his anxiety and a gradual desensitization to whatever stimuli is eliciting the inappropriate behavior.

Aggression toward strangers. This can be the result of territoriality or based

Curbing Aggression

If your Beagle is beginning to act aggressively, you need to take immediate action to correct his behavior. All family members should incorporate the following rules into their daily interactions with your hound. If he has a history of biting, or if he frightens you, we strongly suggest you seek immediate professional assistance. Never take unnecessary chances where safety is concerned.

1. **If Your Beagle Guards an Object, Get Rid of It.** If he growls and becomes aggressive at feeding time, go back and review the discussion on teaching him to accept your presence at the food bowl (see page 30).

2. **Avoid Excessive Petting.** Reserve praise and rewards as reinforcement for appropriate behavior. Excessive praise elevates the hound's social status and sends him mixed signals.

3. **Nothing in Life is Free.** Your Beagle should earn your attention and praise. Insist that he sit to receive petting or treats, sit before going through a doorway, sit to have the leash attached to his collar. Performing simple obedience exercises constantly reinforces your position as the dominant pack leader.

4. **Never Back Down.** Prevention of aggression requires that you never back down from a confrontation with your Beagle. If he growls when you try to remove him from your bed, take his toy, or approach his food bowl, he is asserting his dominance. If you do not follow through with enforcing your commands, you may be inadvertently reinforcing the aggressive behavior.

5. **No Dogs on the Furniture!** This is especially important in cases of dominance-related aggression. By sharing your sofa or bed with your Beagle, you elevate his social standing to that of your equal. Before you realize it he may even think of you as his subordinate.

6. **Supervise Your Beagle with Children.** Never, ever leave your Beagle unsupervised with children, especially those who do not reside in the household. Instruct your children how to behave properly in the presence of a dog, and if they are old enough, teach them how to exercise control through basic obedience commands.

7. **Neuter.** While neutering will not solve all problems, it may help diminish some forms of male aggression. In the multiple-dog household, neutering can also aid in the reduction of dog-aggressive problems.

on fears and anxieties. If Bailey becomes aggressive when placed in a stressful situation, such as at the veterinary clinic or while attending dog shows, he is probably doing so out of fear. Treatment is again going to be focused on reducing his anxiety and desensitization to whatever is triggering the behavior. The territorial Beagle will act aggressively toward strangers who approach him while at home, in the yard, or out for a walk with his family. Your first step in curbing this type of behavior is to train and tighten his response to simple obedience exercises, particularly the *sit, stay,* and *down-stay.* The next step is geared toward repeated exposure to the stimulus (strangers) that triggers your Beagle's aggression. Always take proper safety precautions; keep him on leash, under control, and muzzled if necessary. Counter-condition him to respond to the approach of a stranger by having him sit politely and focus on you. When he responds to your commands, be sure to reward all appropriate behaviors. The stimulus is gradually intensified, until your Beagle indifferently accepts the presence of a friendly stranger.

Dog-dog aggression. Beagles are rarely dog aggressive, but conflicts can occur in multiple-dog households. Most often these are minor, dominance-related incidents. If the occasional confrontation has escalated from being mostly noise to the actual infliction of bodily injury, then it is time to step in and address the problem.

1. Keep collars and leashes on both dogs whenever they are together so that you can take control and separate them should a fight occur.

2. Try to avoid situations that might promote jealousy.
3. Downplay greetings so that your canine companions are not vying for your attention.
4. Remove all possible reasons to fight, such as shared toys and treats.
5. Provide separate sleeping quarters and always feed each individually, in their own private crate.
6. Training and tightening basic obedience commands can also be helpful.

Barking

Barking is a natural means of canine communication. Bailey may bark at passing wildlife, when a stranger enters your yard, or to express some need. His barking is unlikely to be considered a behavioral problem, until it is produced in excess.

Problem barking has a variety of origins. The key to extinguishing the behavior is to determine what stimulus is triggering Bailey's inappropriate vocalizations. If your Beagle is barking excessively, consider the following possible causes:

- He may be trying to communicate to you that he wants something. If he is outdoors, does he have easy access to shade and a fresh water supply? Does he want or need to go out or come in? Or perhaps he has spied a rabbit or the neighbor's cat, and is barking out of hunting instinct.
- Beagles often vocalize when excited and during play. If you have a multiple-dog household, your hound is likely to bark during canine games of "chase" or "keep away."

69

- Some dogs will bark whenever they feel anxious or threatened. Make sure that no one is teasing your Beagle when he is confined outdoors. If he barks and becomes frantic when left alone in his crate, consider the possibility that he could be experiencing separation anxiety.
- The most common cause of nuisance barking is boredom. Bailey may simply be lonely, or he may be barking as an outlet for his pent-up energies. Try to avoid leaving your hound alone in his crate or pen for excessive periods of time. Inappropriate confinement can cause frustration in your Beagle and result in constant barking. Take the time to make sure that he is receiving sufficient physical exercise and mental stimulation.

Exercise. An instinctive and natural behavior such as barking can be quite challenging to control. It may require considerable time, patience, and effort on your part to curb Bailey's inappropriate barking, but through training and behavior modification a solution is possible. If you have not yet enrolled your Beagle in a group training class, now may be a good time to do so. Obedience training can strengthen the bond between you and Bailey, build his confidence, provide mental stimulation, and give him something better to do than bark. Provide Bailey with plenty of exercise. By wearing him out physically, you may find that his barking will subside.

Removing stimuli. For the hound that barks out of fear or anxiety, avoid or remove whatever stimulus is triggering his feelings of tension. Call Bailey to you when he barks and command him to perform an alternate behavior. Reinforce with praise and a treat when he obeys you. Never inadvertently reward the nuisance barking by yelling at him, or by petting and comforting the nervous hound. Praise him only when he is quiet. The use of remote discipline can also be helpful. You may find that using a spray bottle to startle him with a sudden shot of water in the face is effective in deterring him from barking.

"Beagle-proofing" or day care. If you are not at home when the inappropriate barking is taking place, consider *Beagle-proofing* an area of your home. An indoor Beagle may be more content and less likely to disturb your neighbors. You might also be able to arrange for a friend or neighbor to stop by and take Bailey for a midday walk. An alternative approach would be to search out a local *doggie day-care* facility. Unlike a boarding kennel, these training facilities typically provide your Beagle with physical and mental stimulation while in their care.

Debarking. As a very last resort, in cases where all other attempts at curbing the behavior have failed, you might consider having Bailey debarked. A vocal cordectomy (debarking) is a surgical procedure to remove all or part of the vocal cords. It may not stop him from barking entirely, but does significantly reduce the volume of sound. In a situation where you are faced with the possibly of having to give up your Beagle companion because of his nuisance barking, debarking might be an acceptable alternative. Consult your veterinarian.

Bite Inhibition

The next two topics, teaching *bite inhibition* and coping with *inappropriate chewing*, are somewhat interrelated. Puppies especially have a strong urge to mouth items and chew, both to relieve the inflammation and discomfort of teething and also as a means of investigating their surroundings. Until the age of approximately five months, your Beagle puppy will retain his needle-sharp milk teeth. If he is permitted to bite down forcefully on your hands or stocking feet, he can unintentionally inflict pain upon his human companions. This sort of nipping is often play motivated and rarely related to aggression; your Beagle is simply unaware that the pressure behind his biting may cause you discomfort. The solution? You need to teach him to have a *soft mouth*, which means he must learn that it is unacceptable to bite down hard. You should also deny him the option of mouthing or chewing particular items, while redirecting his natural behavior toward more appropriate outlets.

Teaching bite inhibition. Begin by never allowing Bailey to mouth your clothing or hair, because when he does so, you cannot feel how much pressure he is applying when he bites. If he is permitted to bite down hard on human clothing, he is likely to assume that it is also permissible to bite your hands with equal intensity. The most effective method for training Bailey to control the force behind his bite is through direct training involving remote correction. You want to teach your puppy that biting results in his own discomfort. Allow him to take your hand in his mouth, and then wait for him to apply inappropriate pressure. When he does bite down, immediately pinch his upper lip between your thumb and forefinger. Squeeze just hard enough to cause him obvious discomfort, and then release when he reacts by letting go of your hand. You will be using the same hand that is currently in his mouth to do the pinching, so that he is unable to view the source of his pain. He will soon reason that when he bites down with pressure, he experiences pain as a result. Because of the remote correction he will associate the discomfort he feels, not with you, but instead with his own action of biting.

If Bailey is becoming too excited and nipping during play, another method involves simply getting up and walking away. This is the best approach for the younger members of the family to use, since it is not advisable to permit children to dispense physical corrections. Ignore him totally until he settles back down. He needs to understand that if he won't "play nice," you will not play with him at all. Keep in mind that good habits are just as difficult to break as bad ones. Once Bailey has mastered bite inhibition, he will be far less likely to bite as an adult hound.

Chewing

Your Beagle may chew out of necessity, boredom, anxiety, or enjoyment. Remember that when you leave him home alone, there are only so many things he can do to pass the time. During teething a puppy is especially motivated to chew in order to relieve the very real discomfort of his irritated gums. Because chewing is a perfectly natural canine behavior, prevention and treatment of destructive chewing is focused primarily on redirecting your hound's chewing urge toward appropriate outlets. If he is kept entertained with enjoyable chew items, your Beagle will also be less likely to develop into a recreational barker or digger, and he need not become bored or anxious when left home alone.

You should always be firm and consistent with Bailey regarding the type of items you do or do not wish him to chew. When you catch your hound in the act of chewing an inappropriate item, correct with a simple *"No! Drop it!"* Take the object away from him, and replace it with

Chewing is a natural puppy behavior.

something more acceptable. Praise him immediately when he begins to chew on the appropriate item. Chances are the cow hoof or ear you offer will be more enticing than whatever he was originally chewing on anyway. Most hounds catch on very quickly.

Toys. Any toy that you allow Bailey to play with unsupervised should be virtually indestructible and nonconsumable. Beagles can be very tough on their toys! Avoid those cute little squeaky toys made of plastic or vinyl. The ingestion of non-food items could seriously threaten your hound's health. Appropriate chew items for Bailey include cow hooves, smoked cow or lamb ears, and Nylabones. Rawhides can be wonderfully entertaining chews for Beagles, but they must be used with caution since some dogs will attempt to swallow large pieces and can choke or suffer digestive upsets as a result. Consider trying the pressed rawhide treats as a safer alternative to the large, knotted bones. For some hounds, merely providing access to a few safe chew items is sufficient. Others may require repeated corrections and praise in order to develop a habitual preference for appropriate chew items. Until Bailey is reliable, keep all valuables out of his reach and confine him to his crate when you can't supervise him.

Coprophagia (Stool Eating)

Stool eating, also known as coprophagia, is a common behavior among Beagles. You may discover, to your disgust, that

Bailey seems to take great joy in consuming his own feces or that of another dog. Some hounds have a preference for cat feces or manure. I have yet to meet the Beagle that can resist rabbit droppings. Frozen feces, which some owners whimsically refer to as *pupsicles*, are a popular wintertime treat.

1. **Why Do Beagles Eat Feces?** In the past it was theorized that coprophagia was caused by either an improperly balanced diet or poor health; however this conclusion is not supported by the current research. It might be helpful to understand that this is normal behavior when a mother Beagle has puppies in the nest. Newborn puppies require tactile stimulation in order to urinate and defecate. The mother hound then consumes the puppies' excrement, thus maintaining a clean environment for her family. What is somewhat difficult to understand is why other healthy adult Beagles would want to eat feces. It may be deeply rooted in instinctual scavenging behavior. Some hounds may exhibit this behavior in an attempt to gain attention, or Bailey might just have begun consuming stools out of anxiety or boredom. Most often, the motivation for eating feces is simply not known; Beagles just plain seem to enjoy it.

2. **Is It Harmful?** While you may find Bailey's stool eating extremely repulsive, the truth is that consuming his own excrement is relatively harmless. However, in addition to being socially unacceptable, eating the feces of other animals could expose your Beagle to parasites or disease.

3. **How to Stop This Behavior?** The best solution is to closely supervise Bailey at potty time and never allow him to develop the habit. Remove all temptation; keep your yard clean by scooping and disposing of stools promptly. Follow your Beagle outdoors and when he relieves himself immediately reward/distract him with the offer of a tasty treat while you scoop poop. (This method of rewarding the hound for not eating feces worked so well for one owner that her Beagle now points out every stool pile he can find in order to earn his treats!) If you suspect Bailey might be eating feces out of boredom, try enrolling him in training classes and keeping him active. Always make sure the cat's litter box is securely out of reach. Dietary supplements can be used to deter stool eating, but their success has been rather limited. Sprinkling Bailey's food with MSG or garlic might make his feces taste less attractive; the drawback is that this method does nothing to deter him from eating the stools of other animals. There are also products that can be applied directly to the feces, but many hounds quickly become adept at distinguishing between tainted and untainted feces.

Digging

You used to take such pride in your carefully landscaped yard, but lately Bailey has started creating divots here and there, and occasionally a crater or two. How does one stop a hound from digging? It may help to consider the probable cause of your Beagle's digging habit in order to better determine a potential solution. There are many reasons why both wild and domestic canines dig.

■ Hunting instinct can lead your Beagle to dig. Bailey's highly developed olfactory system allows him to detect all sorts of enticing odors. Just imagine the variety of the scents he is likely to discover in your own backyard. He could be digging in pursuit of insects or mice and other rodents, or while exploring an intriguing scent. There is little you can do to effectively dissuade your hound's natural hunting drive, so your best solution may be to try and eliminate whatever animals or insects are attracting Bailey's attentions. Just be sure to use common sense: Avoid the use of chemicals or poisons that could be harmful to the health of your canine companion.

■ If your Beagle is excavating a few big holes in the ground, he is probably digging for shelter. A good hole is the canine equivalent of lawn furniture. He probably finds a hole especially comfortable, keeping him cooler in summer and warmer during less pleasant weather. It is completely natural for wild canines to dig holes to create a secure den. Some individual domestic hounds will also have a strong urge to dig their own personal hole in the ground. Asking Bailey not to have one may be comparable to asking a person to never again sleep in a bed.

■ Digging may simply be a highly enjoyable recreational activity for your Beagle. He might find the scents of the freshly dug dirt and the feel of the earth beneath his paws particularly pleasurable. The best way to deal with this type of digging problem is to create a special, designated area where your hound is permitted to dig to his heart's content!

■ Many cases of problem digging are the result of boredom. Beagles are social hounds with a high degree of pack drive. They need to be included in their family's daily activities. If Bailey's life is lacking in social and mental stimulation, he will probably resort to engaging in a number of inappropriate behaviors to pass the time. Likewise, the hound that has a lot of pent-up energy from lack of exercise may dig as a means of releasing tension.

The first step in addressing digging, as in almost any problem behavior, is to teach and tighten Bailey's basic obedience exercises. Spend quality time with your Beagle. Take him to group classes, keep him occupied, and wear him out. Most dogs like to feel productive; they like to think they have a job to perform. If Bailey is an outdoor Beagle, you may be able to curb his digging by allowing him access to the home, where he can be closer to his human pack members. A doggie door makes the house available to him, while still providing him with ample opportunity to venture outside. If you prefer not to let your hound have the run of the house, you can create a Beagle-proofed area where the doggie door is installed. A gated-off kitchen in which Bailey has access to his crate, a dog bed, water bowl, and safe chew items will work well.

If you have ruled out all other causes, then you probably own a Beagle that just loves to dig! Several common tactics employed to hinder digging include burying bricks or rocks where your hound likes to dig and filling his existing holes with water. Unfortunately, these approaches may make Bailey momentarily contemplate the situation, but are unlikely to extinguish the behavior. The persistent digger will simply search out a new place to dig. The solution might be to provide your Beagle with a nice, sandy area of his own where he is permitted to dig. You can teach him to use the appropriate digging area by calling him over to it, and then digging in the sandpile with your hands. Encourage your Beagle to join in the game and then praise him for digging in the designated location. You might also provide remote rewards by hiding a few choice treats or chew items in the dry sand for him to discover. When you catch him in the act of digging in any inappropriate place, tell him *"No digging!"* and then take him to his spot. When your Beagle begins digging there, praise him profusely.

Fear of Thunder and Loud Noises

When a Beagle reacts in fear, it is usually caused by lack of exposure or an unpleasant previous experience. Some hounds will exhibit fear during a thunderstorm, and yet show little or no reaction at all to other types of loud noises. For this reason, it has been speculated that the hound may be reacting as much to the atmospheric pressure changes during a storm as to the noise itself.

Your Beagle should be conditioned to be comfortable with loud noises from the first day you bring him into your home. If you use stainless steel food bowls, occasionally drop one onto the kitchen floor from a height of several feet. Your puppy might initially be startled, but should soon recover and come to investigate the source of the sound. When his tail comes up and he relaxes, praise and reward him with a treat. If he shows excessive fear of the noise, back off on the volume and begin again with a less startling sound. You can also use your stereo to gradually habituate your hound to a variety of noises. Sound effects CDs are readily available that include such commonly feared noises as thunder, fireworks, and gunfire. By starting at a very low volume, Bailey becomes desensitized to the sounds. Through repetition and a very gradual increase in volume, your Beagle soon learns to react with indifference to loud noises. You may also find it helpful to incorporate playtime and positive reinforcement into these training sessions.

Even if he never seemed to mind storms as a puppy, Bailey may one day begin to develop a fear of thunderstorms. The reason for this is sometimes unclear; it may be rooted in an unpleasant experience. But regardless of the cause, there are several different ways you can help your Beagle to cope with this fear.

1. **Offer Calm Reassurance.** If thunderstorms make you nervous, Bailey may be taking his cue from you. He needs to be reassured that there is nothing to be afraid of. Acting as if the storm is no big deal may be the best approach. Completely ignore the storm and go about your business. Speak to Bailey in a pleasant, upbeat voice and encourage him to go lie down.

Beagles are prone to overexuberance.

or favorite chew item reserved for use only during stormy weather. But at the same time take care not to pet and fuss over your hound in an attempt to comfort him. Such actions could inadvertently reward his fearful behavior.

4. **Desensitize Your Beagle to Loud Noises.** As we discussed earlier, you can modify Bailey's behavior through repeated exposure to a gradually increasing volume of noises. Dim the lights and play recordings of storm sounds. By playing with your Beagle, or putting him through his obedience exercises and then rewarding appropriate behavior, you may be able to teach him to accept and ignore the sounds of a storm.

Jumping Up

Jumping up on people is a natural way in which your Beagle companion may greet you. He is excited and happy to share your company. He may be attempting to reach your face in order to welcome you in the same manner a hound would greet any dominant pack member—with a kiss under the chin.

In order to curtail the jumping, you might try reshaping the greeting behavior. This can be achieved by ignoring your Beagle when he jumps up, and using positive reinforcement when he sits or at least keeps all four feet on the floor. Because jumping up on people normally occurs as a greeting and an attention-seeking behavior, withholding your attention can be an especially effective approach. When you realize your Beagle is about to jump up, simply cross your arms, turn your back

2. **Use the Crate.** If Bailey has a particular safe place, such as his crate, you may find that he rides out the storm better there. He might actually prefer to be in his crate, but instead is following you around because he feels responsible for your protection. Encourage him to go relax in his crate, and you may find that he soon settles down and is more comfortable. The plastic, airline-style crates usually work better as a secure den than those made of open wire.

3. **Provide Careful Positive Reinforcement.** For the Beagle that is only mildly afraid of storms, it can be effective to teach him to associate the changing weather with something pleasant. You may be able to distract him with a fun activity

to him, and walk away. As soon as his feet hit the floor, give him a nose hug and kneel down to his level while praising and allowing him to greet you. You might also decide to incorporate the *sit* command, teaching your hound to always sit politely when greeting people. If he is already in the habit of jumping up to get your attention, you may experience an "extinction burst." This simply means that before your Beagle gets better, he will probably get worse. When the reward for the inappropriate behavior is initially withdrawn, he may try even harder to get your attention. Be persistent; eventually he will realize that jumping on people is an unrewarding behavior.

Another method includes mild correction. If your attempt to sidestep Bailey as he leaps at you fails, then grab his front paws with your hands and hold onto them. Keep him standing upright and slightly stretched out. Since most Beagles do not spend a great deal of time standing on their hind legs, he will soon begin to feel tired and uncomfortable. When he begins to struggle to get down, let go and drop him back into a standing position. Follow up with praise and a scratch behind the ears when he again has all four feet on the floor. He will soon learn that when he jumps up it results in his mild discomfort, but more polite behavior earns him praise and attention, which is what he really wanted in the first place.

Separation Anxiety

Has Bailey become a Velcro hound lately? Does he shadow your every move while you are home, and then become frantic at the first hint of your impending departure? If your Beagle is becoming a basket case every time you leave him home alone, *separation anxiety* may be the problem. Separation anxiety is typically characterized by disruptive behavior when left alone, due to your hound's distress and anxiety about being separated from his pack members. A multitude of undesirable behaviors are associated with separation anxiety. These include destructive behavior, excessive vocalization, inappropriate elimination, attempts to escape confinement, and self-mutilation.

The Beagle that suffers from separation anxiety may exhibit the following symptoms:

- He often becomes distressed or frantic shortly before or immediately following your departure.
- The inappropriate behaviors occur only when he is physically separated from the person(s) he is especially attached to. This could be when you are away from home, or when he is merely confined in a different area of the household.
- He may show an exaggerated greeting response upon your return, and then he shadows your every movement as if he is worried you might leave him again.
- In extreme cases, the anxiety and disruptive behavior may occur even when your hound is left with other human caretakers or canine companions.

Most separation anxiety is rooted in a lack of confidence and security. Your first step in dealing with this problem should be to go back and reinforce all of the dominance and bonding exercises. A

Beagle that completely accepts you as his pack leader should also accept that you will always make wise decisions. If you leave him confined to the crate for short periods of time, he should accept your decision and trust that you are doing what is best for him.

A gradual desensitization to your departure is also necessary.

1. Begin by toning down all greetings and departures.
2. Crate your Beagle for short periods of time while you are at home.
3. Provide him with an especially enticing chew item, to be used only during these training sessions.
4. Leave quietly and without saying anything to him.
5. Gradually increase the amount of time he is left alone. When you do return, don't make a big fuss over him. All but ignore him initially, hang up your coat, and go about your business. Then, a short time later, acknowledge him and kneel down to greet him more warmly.
6. In extreme situations, where you are genuinely concerned that your Beagle may injure himself while you are not home, consult your veterinarian about the option of prescribing antianxiety medications.

Shyness

Beagles are typically possessed of confident, outgoing temperaments, but the occasional individual hound may tend to be more shy and nervous in personality. A rescue Beagle that has been abused, neglected, or simply poorly socialized may be more prone to react in fear to unfamiliar sounds, objects, and people. One of the major concerns, if you own a shy Beagle, is that he could potentially bite as a defensive reaction born out of fear.

It should go without saying that your Beagle is far less likely to react fearfully if he is in the presence of a person he respects as his pack leader. Establish yourself as his *alpha* and your Beagle should feel safe and secure whenever he is with you. Use his basic obedience exercises to provide him with a directed way to behave in potentially distressing situations. Having something to do will help him focus on you and better cope with his anxieties.

The actual method of desensitizing your Beagle to his fears of unfamiliar people or objects is basically the same as that outlined earlier in this chapter for extinguishing aggression toward strangers. Always praise your shy or fearful pet for trying anything new. Encourage him to approach and inspect things on his own accord. Eventually, he should become indifferent about the presence of unfamiliar people or new objects.

Submissive Urination

It is not unusual for Beagles, especially puppies, to occasionally experience submissive or excitement urination. If approached with patient understanding, your hound should eventually outgrow the problem, gaining both confidence and better bladder control as he matures. In cases of either submissive or excitement urination, it is recommended that you consult his veterinarian in order to rule out possible medical reasons for the behavior.

Submissive urination. If Bailey is urinating whenever he feels threatened or dominated, he is reacting submissively. You should understand that this type of response is based on his perception of a threat, and not necessarily based on the actual intention of the approaching person or other canine. He may urinate during greetings or when being disciplined. The urination is frequently accompanied by submissive posturing, such as crouching down with ears lowered, or rolling belly up. You may find that the submissive urination will subside when Bailey becomes more confident. Work on his obedience exercises, gradually introduce him to new situations, and make all of his experiences as positive as possible. Try to avoid intimidating your hound by making alpha eye contact, or hovering over him; instead, get down to his level and greet him with a scratch under the chin. Don't punish or scold him, as this often makes the problem worse. Your Beagle will also benefit from your giving him an exercise to perform as an alternate behavior. Command him to sit as you approach, and then reward him when he obeys.

Excitement urination. This occurs most frequently during greetings or playtime. It is not usually related to a lack of confidence, or accompanied by submissive posturing. Most cases of excitement urination are related to a lack of complete bladder control and seen in hounds that are less than one year of age. Urine may dribble out whenever the puppy becomes too excited. If he suffers from excitement urination, restrict play to outdoors to prevent accidents until he is more mature

and the problem resolved. Keep greetings low key and ignore him until he calms down. Never punish him for this type of urination; it is not an intentional behavior, and the puppy may not even realize he is leaking urine when excited. Again, consult your veterinarian if you have questions or have not yet ruled out a physical cause for the problem.

Tolerance of Children

The special bond between a child and his Beagle can be a wonderful thing. Just as all dogs must learn how to act around children, all children should learn how to act appropriately around dogs. The following guidelines can help your family to nurture a harmonious relationship between Bailey and the children in your household.

■ Never leave your Beagle unsupervised with a child. Young children may unintentionally frighten or injure him. He might feel threatened by a child who chases him or makes sudden moves and high-pitched sounds. Children should be taught to *never* strike your pet, and to lower their voices during play.

■ Always separate your Beagle from children during snack time to prevent the temptation of stealing food. Little fingers are often nipped accidentally by a hound attempting to grab for a tasty treat. The majority of Beagles, no matter how well trained, tend not to look upon children as authority figures. Children are more likely to be viewed as lower-ranking pack members and considered of equal social status by your Beagle. This in part explains why Bailey might challenge a child or steal food from him without a second thought.

■ Bailey should have his own private den, a secure place where he can retreat to rest unmolested. Never allow children to disturb him while he is eating, ill, resting, or otherwise confined to his crate.

■ Every family member—children included—should learn how to control the Beagle using simple training techniques. Even fairly young children can learn how to command a hound to *"Sit!"* and reward appropriate behavior with a treat. Bailey will quickly learn that children are fun, and they dispense lots of yummy treats in exchange for a simple *sit.*

■ If your hound is confined to an outdoor pen, or has access to a fenced yard, make sure that the neighborhood children do not tease him. When dogs

---

A Favorite Game: "Go Fetch!"

Many canine behavior problems develop out of boredom and as a means of releasing pent-up energies. A brisk game of Fetch is one activity you can use to provide your Beagle with constructive exercise and socialization. Hound puppies can learn to perform an informal *retrieve* as young as six week of age. Bailey is likely to enjoy both the attention and mental stimulation provided by this interactive game. Once mastered, the *retrieve* can also be used as a reward and motivator when teaching your Beagle to perform additional behaviors.

1. Begin training the *retrieve* by introducing Bailey to a plush doggie toy or small ball. Plush, squeaky-type toys work well. Encourage him to pounce on the toy and pick it up. Praise your hound and encourage him to return the toy to you.

2. If he does not immediately release it, tell him to *"Drop it!"* and gently remove the toy from his mouth. Make sure he is paying attention and then command *"Go fetch!"* or *"Get it!"* as you toss the toy a few feet in front of him. When he picks it up, again praise and call him back to you excitedly.

3. If your Beagle tries to turn the *retrieve* into a game of "keep away," ignore him and refuse to play. It usually *does* not take long for a pup to realize that the fun continues only if he is willing to bring you the toy to be thrown again.

4. With older puppies and adult Beagles, the plush toy can be replaced with a tennis ball. You may eventually choose to incorporate the elements of a formal *retrieve*, which requires Bailey to sit politely beside you until commanded to *"Go fetch!"* and then sit in front of you when returning the retrieved item.

Beagles are devoted companions.

Children and Beagles share a special bond.

bite children, it is often because they have been tormented beyond endurance.

■ Never play games of dominance such as tug-of-war with your Beagle. If he learns to tug on an item to gain possession, he also may begin to believe that any item he can grab and take away from a child is his.

Preventing aggressive behavior toward children from developing includes early socialization. All family members must learn to handle your Beagle puppy gently and treat him with respect.

1. Teach Bailey to take food without grabbing or lunging by having both adults and children feed him by hand.
2. Don't allow him to chase children or become overly excited during play.
3. Teach bite inhibition.
4. When your Beagle does get too rough or acts aggressively, resist the temptation to physically punish him. End the playtime immediately.
5. Teach Bailey alternate, appropriate behaviors and reward him only when he complies by conducting himself politely.

8 *The Canine Good Citizen*

In recent years, there has been a proliferation of antidog legislation. Signs declaring "No Dogs Allowed!" can be seen in many locations, posted by people who have grown weary of poorly mannered canines and their irresponsible owners. All pet owners suffer the consequences because of those who continue to show disrespect for other people and their property. Only through a continued effort to exhibit

common courtesy and proper canine etiquette can responsible dog owners combat the antidog sentiment within their community.

How can you do your part? Begin by teaching Bailey to behave appropriately in public. A well-mannered dog commands respect from others who are bound to take notice of your polite Beagle buddy. Striving for a properly trained canine companion, always under control, should be the norm rather than the exception. Be a good neighbor. Pick up after your Beagle whenever you walk him in parks or other public places. Remember that dog ownership is both a privilege and a responsibility.

The AKC Canine Good Citizen Program

The Canine Good Citizen program was introduced by the AKC in 1989 to insure the continued acceptance of our canine companions within the community. CGC certification is designed to reward dogs that behave appropriately both at home and as community members. In addition to recognizing well-mannered dogs, the

Pictured is a handsome pair of well-trained hounds.

program also aids in promoting responsible dog ownership.

To receive the CGC award, your Beagle will need to take and pass the ten-item Canine Good Citizen test. Dogs are evaluated on a pass/fail basis, and need qualify only once in order to earn their CGC certificate. Your hound need not even be a purebred to participate; the CGC program is open to mixed or random breds as well.

Preparation

Preparing for the CGC exam is relatively simple. Any well-mannered dog that has mastered the basic obedience exercises of *sit, down,* and *stay* is likely to pass the tests. He must be old enough to have received his protective immunizations, such as vaccination against rabies, but otherwise there is no age requirement; your Beagle is never too young or too old to be a Canine Good Citizen. All exercises are performed on leash and in an informal setting, which takes a lot of pressure off the novice hound and handler. And because the CGC program is designed to show that your Beagle is an appropriately behaved community member, the emphasis is on his reaction to a variety of situations and people rather than flawless obedience.

The CGC program eliminates most of the common excuses for failing to properly train your hound. Teaching your Beagle the basic manners required to pass this test will secure his position as a polite family member. The tests are typically administered by persons with experience in training dogs for Obedience, show, and/or field competitions. When you attend the CGC exam, you will be required to present Bailey's current rabies certificate and any other state or locally required certificates and licenses. You will also need to bring along a brush for the appearance and grooming portion of the examination, and your Beagle must wear a properly fitted flat or slip collar. Special obedience training equipment, such as prong collars or halters, are not permitted. Your hound should be presented on his normal training lead made of leather or fabric.

Once Bailey is responding reliably to the basic obedience commands, and he focuses his attention on you in new situations, you may well be ready to try for his CGC certificate. This can often be accomplished through simple home schooling. If you feel you still need assistance in preparing for the Canine Good Citizen test, many kennel clubs offer special training classes that will help you to teach your Beagle all of the required skills.

The Ten Exercises

Test 1. Accepting a Friendly Stranger

The first exercise is designed to demonstrate that you can maintain control over your Beagle when meeting a friendly stranger. He should remain calm and polite while you greet and shake hands with another person. During this test, the evaluator will approach and speak with you while ignoring your hound, who is expected to hold his position, neither

Meeting new people is fun.

Test 2. Sitting Politely for Petting

The second test begins with Bailey sitting politely at your side. He must allow a stranger to pet him without showing any sign of shyness or resentment. It is permissible for you to use your hands to ease him into a sitting position. The evaluator approaches and asks permission to pet your dog. He will then gently pet Bailey on the head and body, circle you, and walk away. You may speak to your Beagle to reassure him and demonstrate your approval during the evaluation.

1. To prepare for this and the previous test, you will need the assistance of a friend. With Bailey walking or *heeling* politely, approach your friend, and then place your Beagle in a *sit-stay*. Your helper should stand quietly until you feel confident Bailey will hold his position; he may then approach and pet your hound. Remind your Beagle to be steady and then praise and reward him for not breaking from the *sit* while being petted.

2. The next step involves again approaching a second person and commanding Bailey to sit. This time your friend greets you and shakes hands, but leaves without touching your Beagle. As before, praise and reward him for behaving appropriately and remaining steady. Encourage him to focus on you throughout the exercise.

3. Finally, you can practice the actual test procedure by having Bailey sit next to you while a stranger approaches and either greets you and then walks away or asks permission and then pets him.

avoiding nor approaching the second person. Any display of aggression, such as barking or growling, results in failure.

The most difficult part of this test for most Beagles lies in not approaching the evaluator. Beagles naturally tend to want to make friends with everyone they meet. You will need to teach Bailey to wait patiently, and that praise and petting are offered only as a reward for waiting politely in position. If your hound is one of those rare individuals that is either shy or a bit too assertive, then go back to Chapter 7 and review methods for reshaping his problem behaviors. But if Bailey is a typically friendly Beagle personality, you will probably find it most helpful to train for the first and second portions of the CGC test in reverse order.

Grooming demonstrates proper care.

Be prepared to remind your hound to remain in the sitting position until he is completely reliable.

Test 3. Appearance and Grooming

Your Beagle will be examined to determine if he is clean, healthy, and well cared for. The evaluator will use the brush that you provide to gently groom your hound, and will also examine his ears and handle each of his feet. Bailey need not remain in a specific position throughout this portion of the test, but should not object to being handled and groomed by a friendly stranger. You are welcome to talk to your Beagle reassuringly, but may not restrain him during the examination.

This evaluation tests Bailey's willingness to allow someone other than you to handle him when necessary, such as when visiting the veterinarian, at a grooming shop, or attending a dog show. It also demonstrates that you are a responsible owner who takes proper care of your hound. The best preparation is to regularly groom and handle Bailey from the time he joins your family. A quick, daily brushing will keep his coat shiny and clean by removing dust and dander while distributing the natural oils. Also, frequent examination of your Beagle's ears and feet will allow you to detect or prevent many common health problems.

Test 4. Out for a Walk (Walk on a Loose Leash)

Part of Bailey's most basic manners training included walking politely on leash, which is the exact behavior called for in this test. It is unimportant whether or not your Beagle walks on your left or right, or sits when you stop. Your hound is not required to *heel* as in the more formal obedience exercise, but simply to walk along with you at your natural pace. The evaluator will instruct you to turn left, right, reverse direction, and stop while Bailey walks at your side on a loose leash. You are permitted to speak to your hound throughout this exercise and to offer him encouragement. Training your Beagle to walk politely is covered in Chapter 6.

Test 5. Walking Through a Crowd

This is similar to the previous exercise, but this time you and Bailey will walk past a group of three people, some of whom may be accompanied by their own well-mannered canines. It is permissible for your Beagle to show a passing interest in the crowd members, but he should remain under control and not react aggressively nor shy away. Keep your hound close to your side and talk to him, encouraging him to remain focused on you as much as possible. Preparation involves walking Bailey in public places where he may face similar distractions, or practicing polite on-leash behavior with a group of friends.

A well-mannered Beagle is never aggressive toward other dogs.

Test 6. Sit and Down on Command/Staying in Place

In this test, your Beagle must respond to the commands to *sit* and *down,* and then must hold his position until you release him. Rather than using his regular training leash, you will place Bailey on a 20-foot (6.1-m) long line for this exercise. It is permissible to gently guide your hound into the required position, but he must sit and lie down without protest; you may not force him or bait him into position using food bribes. You are permitted to take your time and may repeat commands if necessary. Precise performance is not required, just a demonstration of basic good manners. Once your Beagle is in position, the evaluator will ask you to leave him and walk to the end of the long line. He must wait patiently until you return and give him a *release* command.

Test 7. Coming When Called

Your Beagle is required to come to you when called, in this case from a distance of 10 feet (3 m) away. Command Bailey to *"Wait,"* then walk away while the evaluator distracts him with petting and attention. When you call your hound to come, it is permissible to kneel down and pat your legs or otherwise coax him to you. He is required to approach at least closely enough for you to reach out and touch him, but need not sit in front as is required in the formal obedience *recall*. Training is the same as the basic *recall* discussed on page 58. Further preparation involves practicing the exercise with a friend who will pet your Beagle and potentially provide a mild distraction.

Test 8. Reaction to Another Dog

While walking with Bailey, the two of you meet a friendly stranger who also has a well-behaved canine companion. Your Beagle may show a mild interest in, but should not approach, the other dog. Beginning from a distance of approximately 30 feet (9 m) apart, you and the other owner will approach one another, stop and exchange greetings briefly, then continue on your way for an additional 15 feet (4.6 m) or so.

This test demonstrates that you are able to keep Bailey under control and that he is not dog aggressive. It helps if both dogs walk at *heel* on the left side of their owners and pass toward the outside. Try to maintain Bailey's focus on yourself so that he remains obedient and is not distracted by the presence of another canine.

To prepare for this test, you will need the assistance of a friend and his well-mannered dog. Training begins by placing Bailey in a *sit-stay* at your side while another handler and dog approach and pass within a few yards of you. Gradually, have the other owner and dog pass closer and then stop, until eventually they are able to approach and stop within hand-shaking distance. Next, reverse the exercise so that the second dog and handler team are sitting still while you and Bailey approach to within increasingly closer distances. Finally, practice walking the dogs

Note: To prepare, you need to teach Bailey the three involved obedience commands. Sit was discussed earlier, in Chapter 6. Methods for teaching your Beagle to lie down and stay can be found in Chapter 12, and so are not repeated here.

past one another without stopping, then turn, face each other, and command Bailey to sit. Eventually, you should be able to stop closer and closer together until both dogs are reliable and sitting politely while you stop and exchange greetings.

Test 9. Reactions to Distractions

To pass this exercise, Bailey must demonstrate his confidence and steadiness in the face of distractions. The evaluator will select two separate distractions involving sight and/or sounds that might be startling to your Beagle. Visual distractions may include a person running by or riding a bicycle, or someone on crutches or in a wheelchair. Sound distractions can be anything from a chair being knocked over to someone dropping several heavy books, a slamming door, or a group of people engaged in boisterous conversation. Bailey may show interest, but should not react by becoming overly excited, fearful, or aggressive.

Preparation involves repeated exposure to distracting sights and sounds throughout your Beagle's basic training. Taking him to public places where he is likely to encounter all sorts of distractions is the best way to teach him to ignore them. Work on his obedience exercises until he is able to remain focused and does not become distressed by goings on around him. If he shows fear or defensive aggression in reaction to specific situations, go back to Chapter 7 and work on desensitizing him to the stimulus that makes him uncomfortable.

Test 10. Supervised Separation

This final exercise tests your Beagle's ability to remain calm when he is briefly separated from you. He will be left in the company of the evaluator for three minutes while you are outside of his field of vision. It is permissible for him to move around, but he must not struggle to escape, bark, nor constantly whine and pace. He may show an interest in where you have gone, and mild agitation, as long as he remains calm and polite.

Training Bailey to "Wait" begins by having him sit and then handing the leash to a friend or other family member. Walk a few feet away, and after one minute return and praise your Beagle for waiting patiently. Next, command your hound to "Wait," hand the leash to your helper, and then walk around the corner and beyond Bailey's line of sight. Gradually increase the amount of time he must wait for your return, until he is contently waiting for three minutes or more without becoming anxious.

CGC Certification

All dogs that pass the CGC test receive a special certificate from the American Kennel Club. As of 1999, they also are automatically recorded in the AKC's Canine Good Citizen Archive. Because it is not a competitive event, the Canine Good Citizen program allows everyone to go home a winner!

Where can you go to have your Beagle tested? Your local, all-breed kennel club probably offers Canine Good Citizen testing at least once or twice each year. There are also often additional groups that offer CGC testing, including those devoted to 4-H, therapy dogs, private trainers or groomers, and obedience training clubs. The AKC's Canine Good Citizen Department can provide you with the names of clubs and evaluators in your area.

A Stepping-stone

The CGC award is not an ending point, so much as it is a stepping-stone toward participation in other activities. Many owners find training their Beagle for the Canine Good Citizen program so satisfying that they decide to pursue more advanced Obedience and Agility work. And achieving the CGC certificate is one of the requirements for certification as a registered therapy dog through groups such as Therapy Dogs International.

9 *Therapy Dog Work*

"There is nothing more satisfying than spending two hours at a nursing home and rehabilitation center sharing your beloved, well-trained canine companions with the residents. The joy on the residents' and caretakers' faces as they pet the dogs and have them perform their favorite tricks for them is indescribable. But even more heartwarming is the look on the hounds' faces as they respond to the laughs and hugs from their favorite special people. It is certainly a very touching experience for all involved."—*Marie Morris*

Don't you enjoy the warm feeling of companionship that you get when you give Bailey a scratch behind the ear, to

> **Note:** In this and subsequent chapters, I have incorporated comments from Beagle owners who regularly participate with their hounds in the relevant activities. Personal remarks may be found in quotations, followed by the contributor's name in italics. I hope that these firsthand observations will be of help to you, both in promoting understanding and identifying those activities that you might enjoy exploring further.

which he responds with an enthusiastic wag of his tail and seems to smile back at you? Don't you love watching your Beagle share that same warmth with other people, especially when the simple bestowal of your hound's unconditional affection brings a sparkle of joy to an otherwise dreary day? These are a few of the small pleasures that volunteer therapy dog teams are able to share with persons confined to care facilities such as hospitals, rehab centers, and nursing homes.

The Benefits of Canine-Assisted Therapy

Although dogs have served as valuable companions to humans for thousands of years, it is only within recent history that animal-facilitated therapy programs were developed. Scientists have acknowledged that a direct correlation exists between emotional health and the canine-human bond. Studies have demonstrated that a person holding or petting an animal experiences a lowering of blood pressure and release of tension. A relationship with an animal can be far less threatening than a human-to-human relationship, satisfying the needs for loyalty, trust, and unconditional love. Simply put, canine therapists are able to provide benefits that medical science cannot—they can draw a person out of the isolation of loneliness, relieve depression, and successfully speed up the therapeutic process.

Therapy dogs offer affection and tactile reassurance without criticism. Often deprived of acceptance and love, those who live or must stay in a care facility experience an immediate, positive response to the gentle expression and wagging tail of a therapy Beagle. The owner and dog teams make a significant difference in the quality of life, providing valuable therapy. Participation in canine-assisted therapy is a mutually rewarding experience for the volunteers as well. It can be a pleasure to share the comradeship of your well-mannered Beagle while also providing a beneficial service to the community.

Is Your Beagle a Prospect?

How can you determine if your Beagle is a good prospect for participation in therapy dog work? First, you will need to honestly evaluate your hound's temperament and training and decide if both are up to par. If not, are you prepared to devote the necessary time and effort to work with Bailey until he is sufficiently safe and reliable enough to participate in canine-assisted therapy? The following points are worthy of consideration:

1. Evaluate Your Beagle's Personality. Is Bailey calm and friendly when meeting new people? The patients that your hound will visit must be absolutely safe from potential injury. Therapy dogs need to be extremely forgiving of any pain that might be inflicted on them, whether accidental or intentional. Infirm

Canine therapists offer unconditional affection.

Therapy Beagles must be tolerant and gentle.

hands may pet too roughly or pull at ears and fur. Also keep in mind that many of the people you visit will be in fragile condition. Elderly skin may tear or welt easily, and an affectionate bump by your little hound could topple someone who is unsteady on their feet.

2. How Does Your Beagle React to Unusual Events, Sights, or Sounds?

Keep in mind that Bailey is likely to encounter many new experiences during his visits to a care facility, and you must be able to maintain adequate control over him at all times.

3. Is He Polite and Well Mannered?

Bailey should be able to walk politely on leash and respond to the basic commands to *sit* and lie *down*. Knowing a few simple tricks can also provide entertainment for the residents he visits. Since the therapy routine often involves petting and brushing, your hound should welcome such attentions, even from a total stranger.

Therapy Dog Certification

There are various organizations that certify dogs as pet therapists, including Therapy Dogs International and the Delta Society (for addresses and phone numbers, see page 144). Before being certified, Bailey must pass an evaluation to make sure he can be a safe participant in canine-assisted therapy. The TDI test is virtually the same as the CGC, with the addition of certain situations your hound might encounter during a routine therapy visit.

Therapy dog work is mutually rewarding.

"Once the test is passed, and your Beagle receives his certificate, it's time to go to work. You can either join a group in your area that visits local facilities or you can contact the activities person at an institution near you to see if they would like to have visits from your certified pet therapy dog. Most times they are extremely happy to have a pet volunteer."—*Marie Morris*

Since the term *therapy dog* has become a household word, there is frequent confusion regarding its meaning. Currently, all dogs that are registered with Therapy Dogs International provide emotional service only. This is different from *assistance dogs*, which at times are also referred to as therapy dogs. Assistance dogs would include those specially trained to provide daily service to disabled persons, such as Seeing Eye dogs, hearing ear dogs, and those that aid people in wheelchairs.

10 Hunting with Beagles

While large numbers of Beagles are still maintained by foot packs that hunt in the old British tradition, the vast majority of American hounds are kept as family companions and personal hunting dogs. Small game hunting with Beagles continues to be a popular pastime in certain areas of the United States, with cottontail rabbits and snowshoe hare the primary objective. But it really is not at all necessary to harvest game in order to enjoy venturing afield with Bailey. Anyone can appreciate the skillful work of a Beagle as he unravels the elusive mazes of scent, and thrill to the musical voice of a merry little hound in hot pursuit of his quarry.

Early Field Training

Developing the hunting ability of a well-bred Beagle involves very little actual training. A good hunting hound is born with the driving instinct to pursue his intended quarry, and a strong desire to account for the same. Field training is therefore aimed at providing your Beagle with ample opportunity to express his natural talents and gain experience, while also teaching basic manners and biddability.

Before You Begin...

Field-training your Beagle should never be initiated until the puppy is both physically and mentally ready. It would be unwise to expose Bailey to the hazards of the great outdoors before he reaches at least four months of age and has received a complete series of protective vaccinations, including one for rabies. Experienced field trainers generally agree that five to six months of age is an ideal time frame to begin taking your young hunting prospect afield.

You can begin Bailey's schooling at home using the same bonding exercises and manners training discussed in earlier chapters. Don't be overly concerned that you might spoil your Beagle for hunting by keeping him as a "house pet"; nothing could be further from the truth. Given the same opportunities to run, your family Beagle can become just as efficient a hunting companion as the hound that is housed outdoors, if not better. Socialization and obedience help to shape a cooperative hunting partner. It is far more enjoyable to venture afield with a Beagle that handles easily, hunting with you in the location that you decide is appropriate.

The recall. This is a particularly important lesson to be mastered before you ever consider working with Bailey off leash. In addition to responding to the verbal command (covered in Chapter 6), it is recommended that you also train your Beagle to come to the sound of a whistle or hunting horn. Both of these sounds are sharper and will carry far better than a human voice over distance, during blustery weather conditions, and in areas of thick cover. Begin training by blowing the whistle or horn each time you feed Bailey. He will soon learn to associate the sound with the dispensing of food, a powerful motivator. Once this happens, you can begin to use the whistle to call your puppy to you at other times. Whenever he responds to the sound with a quick *recall*, praise and give him a treat. Repeat this exercise throughout the day. Call your hound to you at unpredictable times, such as when he is busy exploring or engaged in other activities. This training will result in his being much more responsive to handling in the field, particularly when you wish to move off toward a new location or need to call him in at the end of a day's hunt.

Once Bailey is ready to venture afield, there are still several more matters to attend to. Before you head out to begin training, please be sure to consider the following:

■ Check regulations regarding training seasons, etc., with your state game commission or similar wildlife agency. Some states restrict field work during specific seasons in order to prevent dogs from disturbing wildlife that may be mating or rearing young.

Beagle puppies enjoy exploring outdoors.

■ Find a training location and obtain permission to access land that has a good rabbit population. Possibilities to explore include privately owned farmlands, Beagle clubs, sportsman's clubs, military bases, and state or federal public lands, such as parks and game lands.
■ Dress appropriately and have proper equipment for your hound. This includes brush clothes and good boots for you; collar (with ID), leash, fresh water, food or treats, bowls, and a secure, well-ventilated travel kennel for your Beagle.
■ Think safety. Be aware of any natural or environmental hazards. Do not push yourself or Bailey beyond physical limitations. Keep first aid kits handy. Always let someone know where you are training and when to expect your return.

Starting Your Puppy Afield

Starting. This term refers to the initial portion of your puppy's field training, beginning with his first venture afield and progressing to the point where he is able to follow a scent trail with a reasonable amount of control, proclaiming his progress by voice. Just as in basic manners training, you will find that many short lessons are more likely to yield the desired results than an occasional long one. Be careful never to exhaust your young Beagle by pushing him too hard early in his schooling—you want him to enjoy field

work. Patience on the part of the handler is especially important. Some hounds will start rather quickly, opening on scent and trailing at less than six months of age. Others may be a year old or older before they finally settle in and give tongue (vocalize) while hunting.

The free-range approach. Just as in basic training, there is no singular correct way to approach schooling a hound for field work. Opinions vary as to the best methods, and in reality, almost any training arrangement that provides for ample time afield will be successful in bringing along a well-bred hunting prospect. The

This smells interesting!

wide scope of methods used range from the extremes of allowing puppies to run free and hunt at will in a farm environment to more closely supervised and structured field training. The theory behind the *free-range* approach is that Beagles basically train themselves to hunt. Their skills continue to improve as they gain in experience. With no one to distract him from the work at hand, a hound can concentrate on pursuing his quarry without worrying about the location of his handler. Unfortunately, in this day and age, few of us have the luxury of acres upon acres of rural landscape in which to allow our Beagles to run free, and the potential drawbacks to free ranging are numerous. The unsupervised hound may develop bad habits, such as running off game, which might have been promptly curtailed had he been accompanied afield by his handler. It can also be rather difficult business to establish control over a Beagle that is used to simply doing as he pleases—and safety is an ever-present issue.

A starting pen. Some owners feel it is beneficial to introduce their young hounds to the sight and scent of a domestic rabbit during early schooling. The preferred way to do this is in an enclosure that contains one or more tame rabbits, called a *starting pen*. Show Bailey a rabbit and then allow him to engage in a short sight chase. When he loses visual contact with his quarry, your Beagle may initially become confused, but instinct soon kicks in and he should begin to use his nose to investigate the enticing traces of scent. Some handlers will at this point vocally encourage the hound to become excited

and search out the rabbit, while others prefer to remain silent and allow the Beagle to work things out on his own. Teaching your Beagle to respond when you call him to a marked line can have its advantages later on. But there is a fine line between *handling* a hound and *interfering* with his work. Take care not to overhandle Bailey or distract him. Let him search out and jump his own rabbits once he knows what he is looking for. A hunting hound needs to develop sufficient confidence and independence. He should forge ahead into promising cover and unravel the trails left by the quarry without constantly relying on his handler for guidance. If you do not have access to a tame rabbit or starting pen, don't despair—these same lessons can be learned in the field.

Early trips afield. Bailey's first few trips afield will be aimed more at allowing him to become accustomed to the many unfamiliar sights, sounds, and scents than at finding rabbits. As your hound becomes more confident in his new surroundings, allow him to wander around and explore the brush. Sooner or later he is bound to lose contact with you and become distressed at the prospect of being lost. Do not go to him. Stand perfectly still and calmly whistle or call him to you. It may take him a few moments of frantic searching, but he will find his way back to you. Expect to repeat this same process numerous times during those early trips. Eventually, as the puppy learns to use his nose, he will begin to cast about with his head down until he strikes your scent and relocates you on his own.

By being brought along in this manner, he learns to keep a general idea as to your whereabouts while afield, and may develop the good habit of checking back with you at the end of a chase.

During one of these outings, Bailey will stumble upon his first wild rabbit. If he gives chase or shows an interest in the scent trail, that is fine and you may have an easy starter. But don't be too surprised or dismayed if instead your little Beagle stands looking after the departing rabbit in amazement, or shows only a passing interest. Be patient. If after a moment or two he still has made no effort to follow, pick him up and gently carry him to the marked trail. Point your finger to the bed or line where you saw the rabbit and encourage him to sniff about. Do not rush him. Natural instinct will kick in over time and Bailey will eventually take more of an interest in trailing rabbits.

Most veteran field trainers agree that it does little to no harm at all to beat the brush and kick up rabbits for your young hound; a good field Beagle will soon learn to search out and find his own game. Poking around in heavy cover with a walking stick may startle up some rabbits that you can then use for training. Again, call Bailey over to the marked line and encourage him to follow the scent trail. With a little coaching and patience, most hounds soon catch on and will come quickly to your call of *"Tally ho!"* ready to run the line.

Opening. At some point during this period of developing excitement about the pursuit of rabbits, your hound will *open*, or begin to bark, while trailing. Per-

haps the most thrilling part of field training for any handler is hearing his young Beagle give voice for the very first time—Bailey has just realized his scenthound heritage. Once your hound is able to do a fair job of following a scent trail for a moderate distance, while proclaiming his progress by voice, he is now said to be *started*. Further schooling will involve learning to more accurately puzzle out the trail and account for his quarry.

Advanced Field Work

Advanced field work includes schooling your Beagle both solo and with selected brace- or packmates in a way that will cultivate and develop his natural hunting abilities. Each hound is an individual, and Beagles may progress at different speeds and with varying styles of work. Your training program should be developed with this in mind, and adjusted to fit Bailey's needs. The eventual goal is a Beagle that will run his rabbits until they go to ground or are harvested, and in the most efficient manner possible.

Picking Checks

Out of eagerness and inexperience, your young Beagle will reach a point while running where he loses the line of the rabbit. These *checks* frequently occur where the quarry has made a sudden turn, doubled back, or otherwise changed its direction of travel. Give Bailey ample opportunity to work out the check on his own. He needs to learn to be patient and persistent in his work, especially at those times when the job becomes more difficult. Should he seem completely stalled, or begin to lose interest, encourage him to search close to the point of loss. If you are certain of where the rabbit went, you may cast Bailey in that direction to help him relocate the line. Once he strikes the scent, he should set out in the new direction and continue his run. As time goes by, he will learn how to handle checks on his own.

Schooling with Other Hounds

Once Bailey is capable of running a rabbit reasonably well solo, it is time to further his education by introducing him to a bracemate. Ideally, this should be an older hound, one that is very patient and careful in his style of work, and not especially fast. Your young Beagle can gain experience and develop further accuracy in trailing by running with high-class company, but be wary of making the mistake of bracing him with hounds that are too fast, wild, and faulty; this is a surefire way to spoil your young hunting prospect by causing him to become overly competitive and sloppy in his work. In his attempt to keep up with the faster Beagle, Bailey may learn to cheat and cut corners. He is unlikely to have much opportunity to contribute to the chase, or to work out the line for himself.

Experienced trainers advise that you start your Beagle solo, and continue to run him alone for approximately the first

Pictured is a cooperative hunting pack at work.

three months of training. Once he has opened and is fairly accomplished at following a scent trail, introduce the bracemate. Make sure that this running partner is one your young hound can beat on occasion, taking the lead when the scent is good and the line not too difficult. On the tough checks the more experienced hound offers aid in regaining the line, and teaches Bailey a lesson in persistence. Your Beagle will also learn to hark in and cooperate with his bracemate when the other finds the scent first, a valuable trait when he runs in field trials or with a hunting pack later on. Once Bailey is capable of picking his own checks and can keep a run going in a steady fashion, withdraw any bracemates and again work him solo. He needs to develop a certain amount of confidence and independence so that he will not be easily led astray by more faulty

Beagles have been used to pursue all sorts of game, including roebuck.

packmates when he is in control of the line. By two to three years of age, your hunting Beagle should be pretty much set in his running style, and can safely run with a brace and packmates of varying skill without a great deal of concern regarding their impact on his abilities.

Gundog Beagles

The *gundog Beagle* might well be termed the workhorse of the breed. Rabbit hunting is a part of our American heritage, and continues to be a popular sporting activity even today. The primary task of a gundog Beagle is to locate small game and bring it out of cover and within range of the hunter's gun. He can also be taught to retrieve, relieving you of the necessity to

venture into heavy brush in order to recover harvested game. While their primary quarry is the rabbit or hare, many Beagles do equally well at trailing and flushing pheasants or other game birds. Packs of Beagles are also occasionally kept for the purpose of pursuing the fox, although most American hunters would consider fox and deer to be *off game*. In other countries, the Beagle has been used to hunt a variety of additional game animals, including roebuck and even wild pigs.

Schooling your hound to be a useful gundog varies little from basic field training, except that the hound must remain steady when shot over. Introduction to the sound of gunfire should be approached with care, or the result may be a *gun-shy* Beagle. Perhaps the worst thing you could possibly do is to haul Bailey out into the backyard and then fire a shotgun at close range; of course the sudden loud noise and ringing in his ears is going to startle him! There really is little point in shooting over your puppy until such time as he can do a fairly good job of running his own rabbit and is well started in the field. Instead, early conditioning should focus on desensitizing him to loud noises of various kinds. This may include hearing muffled gunfire from a distance. Wait until you are on an actual hunting excursion before firing a gun at closer range. On the first occasion of his being shot over, your hound is then more likely to merely hesitate. He may look to you for assurance that all is well, and then resume the chase at hand. If you have taken care to wait for a clear shot, and successfully harvested a rabbit, allow Bailey to trail right up to where the rabbit is lying. Praise him and encourage him to sniff at and perhaps even gently mouth the rabbit. Let your Beagle know in no uncertain terms that he has done well and you are very pleased with his performance.

Beagle Field Trials

Competitive field events provide an excellent opportunity to observe hunting Beagles at work, performing their intended function with (in most cases) agility and efficiency of movement. The field trials also aid in promoting and preserving the historic working qualities of the breed.

AKC Field Trials

There are currently four basic formats of AKC Beagle field trial competitions: Brace, Small Pack, Small Pack Option (SPO), and Large Pack on Hare (LPH). Trials are held separately for all-age Beagles, and also for younger hounds, called *derbies*.

In all of the AKC Beagle field trial events, judges are instructed to keep the original purpose of the breed constantly in mind. The hounds are to be credited principally for their positive accomplishments. Credit is earned for searching ability, pursuing ability, accuracy in trailing, proper use of voice, endurance, adaptability, patience, and determination, proper degree of independence, cooperation, controlled competitive spirit, intelligence displayed when searching or in solving problems encountered along the trail, and success in accounting for game. Faults, mistakes, lack of accomplishment, and

apparent lack of intelligence shall be considered demerits and shall be penalized to whatever extent they interfere with or fail to contribute to a performance.

Brace format field trials. During these trials the Beagles are run as braces or trios. The current trend in judging brace trials has been to place emphasis on the hunting style and accuracy of the hound. Traditional Small Pack trials are also offered, with the primary difference being in procedure only. These formats favor a slower, more methodical working hound that proceeds carefully from track to track in pursuing his quarry.

Small Pack Option field trials (SPO). These are trials in which the Beagles are required to be cast to search for game and demonstrate that they are not gun-shy. This format tends to more closely simulate actual gun hunting with a pack of Beagles, and the emphasis is on accomplishment. SPO Beagles usually display more speed and a keen desire to overtake and account for their quarry. Hounds must be scored on searching ability—in addition to accuracy in trailing—and tested for gun-shyness in all classes.

At Large Pack on Hare Trials (LPH). At these trials the quarry of choice is the hare. All entries are cast as one large pack, but may be split at the option of the field trial committee if entries exceed 25 starters in number. Due to the difference in habitat and running style of the hare, the LPH trials may favor a fast, big-running hound that reaches out a bit further on the checks; emphasis is on accomplishment and accounting for the quarry.

Points. In order to become an AKC Field Champion of record, a Beagle must have won a minimum of three first places and 120 points in classes with not less than six starters through competition at AKC-licensed or member field trials. Points awarded are based on placement and the number of hounds in competition.

The preceding summary is just the tip of the iceberg. Further information regarding the AKC Beagle field trials, and the complete rules and regulations, can be accessed on-line at *http://www.akc.org/dic/events/perform/beagspft.cfm* There are also a multitude of additional Beagle per-

Numbering a field trial entry for identification.

formance events sponsored by other registries and associations of Beagle clubs, such as the ARHA (American Rabbit Hound Association), UKC (United Kennel Club), and UBGF (United Beagle Gundog Federation).

The NBC Triple Challenge

The NBC Triple Challenge event was initiated for the purpose of recognizing and promoting the complete, versatile Beagle. The challenge consists of a weekend of competitions, during which the hunting talents of the individual hound are evaluated (through a brace format field trial), as well as his ability to contribute to the work of a pack afield (during a three-hour stakes class where all entries are hunted as one large pack). Additionally, the qualities of conformation, movement, condition, soundness, and temperament are judged in a conformation show.

Awards are based on a combined score earned through competition in all three phases of the event (field trial, stakes class, and show). Points earned are based on the placement received in each phase of the event, and hounds are required to enter and complete all three phases of competition. The NBC Triple Challenge also serves a very valuable purpose: It brings together representatives of the various factions within the breed at one location, thus opening up the lines of communication.

11 *Traditional Foot Packs*

" ...When I heard Brandy open with that electrifying bawl, as if she had just seen the devil, I knew that we would have a good day's hunting! Soon Bourbon's deep voice joined the cacophony of Raspberry's high chop, Rebel's long yell, Samson's hoarse cry, and Radish's bell-like note. And when Gunsmoke, Relish, Burgundy, Kipling, and Crackerjack joined in, along with Blue's bass tones, they sounded like all the bells in all the towers pealing with joy and excitement! I doubled the horn and we were off to the races.

"About two fields later, as I leaned against a tree, praying for a check so I could catch up with the hounds and catch my breath, a gentle wind blew little yellow leaves like snowflakes across my vision. I thanked God for bringing me to this time... this day... these Beagles. If Beethoven had experienced the pleasure of a hunt like this, he surely would have composed a Tenth Symphony!"—*Wanda T. Sanders Borsa, Joint Master and Huntsman, Holly Hill Beagles*

Organized hunting with a pack of well-matched Beagles can be a thrilling experience. It provides an opportunity to spend a day afield, relishing in the natural beauty of our environment. And for the hound enthusiast, there is nothing else quite like the sight and sounds of an efficient pack of Beagles working cooperatively to account for their quarry.

The British Tradition

Foot hunting with packs of Beagles or Basset Hounds is a traditional sporting activity brought over to this country from Britain. Hunting in an organized pack differs substantially in style from the running of hounds at field trial events or for the gun. Pack work requires a high level of cooperation, featuring anywhere from two couple (four hounds) to upwards of twenty couples of Beagles that are closely matched in both running style and speed. In traditional foot hunting, the hounds work together as if they are one. No single hound is expected to do all the work, but rather, each contributes something unique to the quality of the run. Ideally, the Beagles should work as such a tightly knit group that you could "throw a blanket over the entire pack." While the British packs historically pursued the European hare with the intent to overtake and capture their quarry, American packs are

Holly Hill Beagles—First-Place Three-Couple Pack, 1995.

mines the area to be hunted, casts the hounds, and then signals to and encourages the pack both by voice and use of the horn. Traditional attire for the hunt staff consists of the standard green coats with velvet collars trimmed in the distinctive colors of the pack, white pants, and a white shirt with stock or tie. This livery allows for easy identification of the hunt staff, even at a distance.

hunted simply for the pleasure of the sport. Rarely is the quarry harmed, and the chase quite often ends only when the rabbit grows tired of the game and goes to ground. Typical quarry in the United States is the cottontail rabbit, but some packs also pursue the hare (native snowshoes or introduced European hare) or jackrabbit.

The Hunt Staff

The hunt staff includes the huntsman, who carries the horn and controls the hunt, and several *whippers-in* who act as assistants. It is the job of these whips to help keep the pack members together during the hunt, to alert the huntsman to any problems, and to call or signal when the quarry is viewed. The huntsman deter-

The Hunting Season

The hunting season for organized Beagle packs usually begins in October of each year with a formal "opening day hunt" including the traditional blessing of the hounds by a priest. A *fixture card* announces the dates for additional meets, which are held primarily on weekends and holidays from fall through early spring, at the discretion of the master. Many packs also hold a "puppy show" and "hunt tea" as part of the opening day festivities. The tea is often more of a social lunch or light dinner put on to provide refreshment for guests who follow the hunt.

The appeals of organized *beagling* are many. Some enjoy following a pack merely for the exercise; others find fascination in watching the hounds puzzle out the mazes of tenuous scent. For many, it is the social aspects of the sport that are especially attractive. Beaglers form a happy fraternity, linked together by their love of the chase and shared days afield. Foot hunting has often been called the "poor man's foxhunting"; following the Beagles does not require a deep pocket. Then there are those who discard the role of spectator to take on the responsibilities of master, huntsman, or whip; they give up their leisure time to become totally absorbed participants in the sport. In exchange, these devoted beaglers receive the satisfaction that comes from working closely with the hounds and sharing in the accomplishments of their pack.

Building a Pack

Packs of Beagles may be privately owned and maintained, or supported by subscriptions. The *master* is the person responsible for all decision making regarding maintenance and breeding of the hounds, and may or may not also act as huntsman. Each individual pack establishes its own territory or *country* over which it has gained permission to hunt regularly and that is well-suited habitat for the quarry of choice. Often, this same country is occupied by an organized foxhunt, and special permission is granted the foot Beagles to share hunting privileges. Proper maintenance of a pack of hounds can be costly; annual subscriptions paid by those who enjoy following the pack can help to meet expenses.

The Hounds

Assembling a good pack of Beagles is easier said than done. One does not simply gather into one's kennel a pack of 20 or 30 hunting hounds and expect them to provide excellent sport. Establishing a successful foot pack requires a great deal of knowledge and effort.

Unloading the hounds for a day's sport.

The Warrington Foot Beagles heading home.

In establishing a new pack, you will save yourself a great deal of work by beginning with two to four couples of hounds drafted directly from established hunting packs. Since no huntsman would draft his best hounds, these Beagles will be far from perfect, but are at least already trained to the horn and experienced in the field. It is highly desirable for foot packs of Beagles to be *level*. This implies that the individual members of the pack should be as closely matched as possible regarding size, color and markings, speed, and running style. Quality of conformation and soundness of the individual hounds are also desirable if they are to provide a day's sport afield.

Obedience and manners are important aspects of an organized foot pack. Hounds must be capable of being *walked out* for exercise during those times of the year when hunting is restricted. They should likewise pack up and walk politely with the huntsman when moving off to a meet and when returning to the hound trailer at the conclusion of the hunt. The huntsman must establish from the very start a bond of mutual trust and understanding with his hounds. By training for and demanding steadiness and biddability when at exercise and in the kennel, a pack will also be steadier in its work afield. All Beagle packs are trained to respond to a standard set of commands and horn signals. This allows a drafted hound from one pack to adjust rather easily to hunting cooperatively with his new packmates, as he has already been schooled in the fundamentals.

Following an Organized Pack

For the majority of us, our participation in organized beagling will be restricted to the role of followers. The first step is to obtain information regarding those Beagle packs that are located within reasonable driving distance of your home. This can be done by contacting the National Beagle Club of America (see page 143 for information) and requesting the current roster of recognized packs. Contact the master to find out where and when the next meet is scheduled to take place, and then plan on arriving a good deal earlier than the advertised time. If you are following a subscription pack, you may be required to pay a *cap,* a contribution paid by nonsubscribers to help with the expenses of the hunt.

The National Beagle Club of America

The parent club under which all organized foot packs are registered in the United States is the National Beagle Club of America. The NBC also maintains a stud book for hounds entered into the organized foot packs, and sponsors biannual pack trials for Beagles and Basset Hounds. If you are seriously interested in starting your own foot pack, you will find that the pack membership of the NBC is typically ready to help by providing draft hounds at low cost. Rules regarding registration and other details can be obtained by contacting the club secretary (see Useful Addresses and Literature, page 143).

12 *Competitive Obedience*

"It is a general belief among certain Obedience professionals that Beagles are a difficult breed to train. I believe that if you have a good attitude, lots of patience, consistency, and a sense of humor, anything is possible. Beagles have competed successfully in the Obedience ring at all levels. The competitors have been both field and show types, young and old. There really doesn't seem to be any difference in their abilities as long as certain basic principles are addressed. Just keep practicing, but above all, remember to have fun with your Beagle! If you do this, competing in the Obedience ring can be a very rewarding experience. It's a terrific feeling to successfully show a nontraditional breed in Obedience competition. It's very impressive when a Beagle enters the ring and does an exceptional job."—*Marie Morris*

AKC Obedience trial competitions first began in 1933 and are open to dogs of all recognized breeds. The purpose of these trials is to demonstrate the usefulness of our purebred dogs as companions to their human families. The dog and handler teams are not judged in comparison to one another, but are evaluated on the basis of how accurately they perform a preset series of exercises. Your hound should also demonstrate his willingness to obey, and a smooth and natural performance is preferable to one of absolute, mechanical precision. Each entry receives a point score based on performance. Those that score the required minimum, without being disqualified during any single exercise, earn a *leg* toward their Obedience title. The highest-scoring dogs in each class division also receive awards.

Even if your Beagle is not AKC registered, he can still compete in performance events such as Obedience and Agility by obtaining an ILP (Indefinite Listing Privilege) number from the American Kennel Club. Likewise, hounds that are excluded from the conformation ring, due to disqualifying faults or neutering, are eligible to participate in Obedience trials and earn titles. Here the focus is on training and the accuracy of your hound's performance while completing a specific series of exercises, not on what he looks like or his potential for breeding.

Commands and Signals

"Beagles are very sensitive by nature. Because of this you can use your voice as

Retrieving over a hurdle.

a great way to cue the hound. Beagles are close to the ground—most of the time all they see are the handler's feet; therefore, use your feet as a cue. Leave with the left foot when you want the hound to follow and leave with the right foot when you want the hound to stay."—*Marie Morris*

There are specific, accepted verbal and hand signals that are commonly used for each of the standard Obedience commands. If you intend to participate in formal, competitive Obedience, it is important to become familiar with the commands and rules for each exercise before you begin to train your dog. Make sure that you understand what actions will be penalized and what you can or cannot do while in the ring. You will not want to disqualify your hound through handler errors such as giving a double

command—verbal and signal—when it is not allowed. Details regarding rules and deductions can be found in the AKC Obedience Regulations booklet. Single copies may be obtained free ($1.00 charge for multiple copies) by writing or e-mailing a request to the American Kennel Club.

Vocal Obedience Commands

When choosing vocal Obedience commands, it is important to keep in mind that none of your commands should sound similar to the words used for corrections (*"No!"* or *"Arrh!"*). By choosing only one correction command, the chance of this occurring will be significantly reduced and Bailey should respond more reliably. Keep the number/variety of different voice commands down to a minimum. Many of the commonly used commands were explained in Chapter 4. Additional formal Obedience commands include the following:

■ *"Stand"* means to stand still and remain steady in the *heel* position. It is used during the Obedience exercise of *Stand for Examination*.

■ *"Drop"* is sometimes used by handlers in place of the *down* command. It means *drop* or *lie down* in position. This may be used during the *drop on recall* and *long down-stay* exercises.

■ *"Over"* is the command used for jumping over the directed obstacle and then returning to sit in front of the handler. You will use this for such exercises as the broad jump, high jump, and directed jumping.

■ *"Fetch"* indicates that your Beagle should go and get the thrown, hidden, or lost article with your scent on it and bring it back to the *sit in front* position. This command is used for all retrieving exercises and during *scent discrimination.*

When Bailey hears you using any of these formal Obedience commands, he should understand that you are working and expect his undivided attention. Only upon your issuing the release command of *"OK!"* should your Beagle relax and break position.

Nonverbal Signals

Nonverbal signals can be any clue that alerts your Beagle to what is coming next.

Experienced handlers use their feet, eyes, and general body position to communicate with their dog, in addition to the actual commands given by voice or hand signals. Response to hand signals will be tested during the Signal Exercises, should you and Bailey ever venture so far as to compete at the Utility level. Again, be sure you are thoroughly familiar with the rules before using signals in competitive Obedience. Signals in the ring are permitted only at specific times and must be completed in a precise manner.

Training Classes

Participation in a formal training class is an important step toward preparing Bailey and yourself for competition in Obedience trials. It simply is not possible to simulate the many distractions provided by other handlers and dogs while working solo at home. Attending classes will also allow you to take advantage of the knowledge and expertise of an instructor and other handlers with a wealth of combined experience, and most clubs have their own training equipment, including regulation high and broad jumps, which class members are welcome to use during training.

Organizations that may be able to help you with preparing your Beagle for competitive Obedience include Obedience Clubs and All-Breed Clubs—those devoted to both conformation and Obedience or performance events. Be aware, however, that the majority of Beagle clubs are currently focused on hunting and field trial work only.

Home Schooling

Obedience Exercise Tips

Special thanks to Marie Morris for providing these tips for home-schooling your Beagle for competitive Obedience. Marie is the trainer/owner/handler of a pair of Beagles that have competed quite successfully in the Obedience ring (and also participate in Agility and Therapy work): Inspector Quincy, CD, CGC, TDI, and Brushyrun Twindale's Falcon, CD, CGC, TDI.

General Advice

- Use your Beagle's special training collar during all training sessions. Make sure it is positioned on him correctly. The end attached to the leash should come over, not under, his head as he walks on your left.
- Keep the sessions short (15 minutes).

Step off with your left foot during heeling.

- Use Reward (food, praise) and Correction (voice and a mild tug on collar).
- Start from the *heel* position with the hound sitting on your left.
- Always leave on the left foot when you want the hound to *follow* (*go* foot).
- Leave on the right foot when you want the hound to *stay* (*stay* foot).
- Say *"OK"* as a release from any exercise.
- Don't forget to encourage and praise, especially during the learning phase.

Heeling on Lead

Start from the *heel* position and make sure your Beagle is paying attention to you. Talk to him or encourage him with a treat to begin training. Leave with your left foot as you say *"Heel."* Remember, Beagles are small and see your foot as a cue. If the hound does not respond immediately, give a mild tug with the lead. Praise as soon as he begins to move forward. When training, encourage your hound with your voice as you go along to keep him moving.

Sit at Heel

When you stop, say *"Sit."* Pull up on the leash. If he doesn't sit, reach down and push on his rump as you pull up on the collar. Do not repeat the *sit* command; just say *"Good pup"* as he begins to sit. In time he will automatically sit when you stop. Praise him! If he sits crookedly when you stop, anticipate this problem and reach down and guide him into a straight *sit* just as you halt. That will keep him from swinging his hips out.

Figure 8 on Leash

Before actually doing the Figure 8, practice making small circles in alternating directions (going around an old hula hoop on the ground helps this exercise). When going counterclockwise, the dog must learn to slow down; when going clockwise, he must speed up. When he has learned to make good circles you can proceed to doing the Figure 8 around cones. The hardest part is to get the hound to change speed as he circles the posts. Talk to him and encourage him to slow down and speed up as necessary.

Stand for Examination

To teach this, kneel next to the hound as he sits. Say *"Stand"* and with your right hand pull forward on the collar to make him get into position. When he stands, put your left hand under his belly and rub. Praise as he stands. After he can do this reliably, tell him to stand. Use the hand signal and verbal *stay* command, and then move in front of the hound. If he stays, return to *heel* position and praise. The next time try to circle him. Finally, tell him to *"Stand," "Stay,"* and then move in front as someone touches him. Then return to the *heel* position. Tell the hound *"OK"* to release him from the exercise, and praise for a great job. In

time increase the distance between you and your Beagle to about 6 feet (1.8 m) while he is being touched.

Heel Free

This is taught in much the same manner as the *heel on leash*. Don't even attempt this exercise until your Beagle is *heeling on leash* with very few problems. If you do he will become totally confused and you will have no control because there is no leash. Since there is no leash you must spend a great deal of time encouraging him and keeping his attention. As soon as he begins to lose attention and wander, reattach the leash and return to *heeling on leash!* In the beginning you may only be able to leave him off-leash for a few steps. If he stays with you, praise him; if not, return to the leash.

Recall

This exercise is taught in three stages: the *stay, come,* and *finish.*

1. Start with your Beagle in the *heel* position with him sitting on your left. Begin training for this exercise by giving both a hand signal and voice command to *"Stay."* (**Note:** Never precede this command with the hound's name; save the use of his name for any action that requires forward movement.) Step right in front of him, wait a second or two, then return to the *heel* position. Say *"OK"* to release him and praise him. Keep repeating this, and as time goes on increase the length

Home Schooling

of time you stand in front of him. After your Beagle is reliably staying in this position, increase the distance between you and him, using a long line and holding only the loop at the end. If he breaks position, grab the end of the training collar and place him back into the proper position. Don't repeat the *stay* or *sit* commands. Just praise him as he makes the correction. When he will stay while you go to the end of the long line, begin introducing the *come* command.

2. Again, start in the *heel* position. Give a firm *stay* command. Walk to the end of the long line, turn, and face the hound. Give either a hand signal or say his name and *"Come."* When he responds and comes to you, grab the end of the training collar and ask for a *sit in front*. If he does this, praise him. If he does not respond to the *come* command, give a mild tug on the long line and praise him as he approaches. If your Beagle does not *sit in front*, grab the end of the training collar and pull up, making him sit. Keep repeating until the hound has learned the *stay* as well as the *come* and *sit in front* aspects of this exercise.

3. When your Beagle has learned to do the first two parts of the *recall*, then introduce the *finish*. Tell the hound to *"Stay."* Leave him and ask for him to *"Come."* After he *comes* and *sits*

in front, take the end of the training collar in the left hand. Tell your Beagle to *"Finish"* and give a firm hand signal with the right hand. Switch the leash to the right hand, step back with the right foot, and pull the hound around your body. When he is behind you, switch the leash to the left hand, move the right foot forward, and lead him into a *sit* in the *heel* position. When he does this, praise him lavishly. Keep repeating this part of the exercise until your Beagle does the *finish* without much guiding from you. Remember to praise! Eventually you will be able to do this off leash.

Long Sit

If your Beagle has already learned to sit while practicing *heeling*, just ask him to *"Sit."* Give the command *"Stay"* and step in front. Repeat this and, as he learns what you want, increase the distance between you and the hound and increase the length of time he must stay in the *sit* position. If your Beagle breaks, return, stay in front of him, and put him into the correct position by pulling up on the end of the training collar to make him sit. Do not repeat either the *sit* or *stay* command, just praise him as he makes the correction and leave when he is properly positioned. As you start training for this, keep the distance and time short. Remember, you want your Beagle to succeed, so only go as far away and for as long as he will successfully stay in position.

Long Down

To teach your Beagle to go down, kneel next to him with your left arm over his back, holding onto the end of the training collar. With the right hand, point to the ground and tell him *"Down."* If he goes down, praise him. If he doesn't, take your right hand and sweep his front legs out from under him. Don't repeat the *down* command; just praise him as he is going down. Once he is down, say *"Stay"* and hold him in position. Do this for a few seconds, then release him *("OK")* and allow him to relax. Repeat this procedure until he goes down when you give the command and stays there for a few seconds. Later, give the *down* command and walk in front of him. Stay close to begin, but with time increase the distance between you and him. Finally, increase the length of time your Beagle will stay down while you are across the room for at least several minutes. If he breaks, return, stay in front of him, and put him into the correct *down* position by pulling down on the end of the training collar to make him go down. Do not repeat either the *down* or *stay* command. Just praise him as he makes the correction and leave when he is properly positioned. When he stays down return to the *heel* position, praise him while he is in the *down* position, and say *"OK"* to release him.

Gently lift your Beagle's front legs...

...and ease him into the down position.

Classes and Titles

Novice classes. These are open to those dogs age six months or older that have not yet earned any Obedience title. Bailey may acquire his Companion Dog (CD) title by earning three *legs* in the Novice ring. A leg or *qualifying score* is achieved by earning more than 50 percent of the available points in each exercise and a final score of 170 or more points during a single regular class at an AKC Obedience trial. Each title must be earned before moving on to the next level of competition. The Novice exercises include *Heel on Leash and Figure 8, Stand for Examination, Heel Free, Recall, Long Sit (across the ring, one minute),* and *Long Down (across the ring, three minutes).*

Open classes. These are for dogs seeking to earn the Companion Dog Excellent (CDX) title. The Open exercises include *Heel Free and Figure 8, Drop on Recall, Retrieve on Flat, Retrieve over High Jump, Broad Jump, Long Sit (out of sight, three minutes),* and *Long Down (out of sight, five minutes).*

The Utility classes. These are the most challenging level of competitive Obedience. Bailey may earn his Utility Dog (UD) title by earning three legs in the Utility ring. Additionally, he may earn a Utility Dog Excellent (UDX) title. This requires ten legs; each leg toward a UDX requires that the dog receive a qualifying score in *both* Open B and Utility B at the same show. The Utility exercises include *Signal*

Scent discrimination is a Utility exercise.

Exercise, Scent Discrimination #1 (leather articles), Scent Discrimination #2 (metal articles), Directed Retrieve, Moving Stand and Examination, and *Directed Jumping.*

The ultimate achievement. In formal Obedience, the prefix title of Obedience Trial Champion (OTCH) is the ultimate achievement. Bailey must earn a total of 100 points through placements of first- or second-highest scores in Open and Utility (in accordance with published AKC point schedules) and meet further specific requirements as outlined in the Obedience rulebook.

Attending an Obedience Trial

Jumps are used in both Obedience and Agility.

Once Bailey has mastered the basic exercises, and performs them well during his group training classes, you may feel the time has come to test his obedience at a trial. The best way to begin is by attending a fun match or sanctioned trial event. These are less formal events at which placements and ribbons are awarded, but no credits are given toward earning Obedience titles.

While regular Obedience competition begins at the Novice level, most matches also offer a Sub-Novice class in Obedience.

Sub-Novice generally includes the same exercises that you and Bailey will encounter in the Novice class, but all are performed with the hound remaining on leash. This can be reassuring until you are more confident about his reliability under varying situations. When Bailey is performing well at matches, seek out and enter a licensed Obedience trial or two. You can learn about upcoming dog events through either the AKC events calendar, your local dog club, or the many licensed dog show superintendents.

13 *Tracking*

"Imagine yourself outdoors in a wide green field, the sun warm on your back, a cool breeze blowing. Your eyes are focused on your Beagle, who is happily following her nose along a hidden track while you are keyed into her slightest movement. Your hound's nose goes down and her shoulders lower slightly as the leash slips through your fingers until there is enough line let out. You allow your dog to lean into the harness and then you begin to follow. Only your Beagle knows the location of the invisible trail that will lead you to find the article waiting at its end. You cradle the tracking leash lightly in your left hand, at chest level, so that the slightest change in tension allows you to know what your dog is thinking.

"As she approaches what you later realize is a turn in the track, her head lifts slightly, then dips again toward one side. Your hound circles briefly before turning to continue down the next leg of the track. Another head tilt to one side, then the other, and you presume that your Beagle has just successfully passed a spot where a deer may have crossed through the tracking field earlier that morning. Now she's back on the track again, and has started to pull forward slightly. You trust that she is right and you follow. A few more yards, then another turn... a straight run halfway across the small field... another turn... After a very short 10 or 15 minutes, your hound paws at something lying on the ground. The glove! She's found the glove."—*Diane Wiest*

Tracking is one of the few activities where your dog is the expert. During Obedience or Agility work, the human team member is the one in control, the one who interprets the rules and makes the decisions. But during tracking you must place your full trust in Bailey's ability to puzzle out the trail. It is impossible for a human handler to truly comprehend the intricacies of his canine's scenting capabilities; therefore, success in tracking depends greatly upon your ability to accurately read your Beagle's body language, interpret what he is experiencing, and follow or hold back accordingly.

Fundamentals of Scent

Every canine is naturally endowed with the abilities to distinguish different scents and to follow a trail. Bailey is said to be *tracking* whenever he follows the scent trail left behind by a human or other animal that passed along a specific route. While we can present many theories regarding the elusive subject of scent, only the dog himself knows exactly *how* he deciphers a track.

The canine ability to discern *scent* is highly unique and should not be confused with our own human sense of *smell*. Your Beagle's scenting ability not only involves a keener olfactory system, but also the ability to detect specific scents even in the presence of strong odors that for a human would obliterate our ability to smell anything else. While it may be interesting to speculate on whether a trail is recognized by your hound due to the scents of crushed vegetation, disturbed earth, a scent left behind by the track-layer's shoes, or a combination of factors, it adds little to our understanding of how to better prepare Bailey for a tracking test. It will suffice to know that there are two types of trails: ground trails and airborne trails. Your hound is highly aware of both. The airborne trail is created by scent that has been left in the atmosphere and carried downwind to be deposited on the ground, or higher objects such as a fence line or shrubbery. Your Beagle is also able to distinguish between the differing scents of individuals. This may explain in part why a pack of well-bred hounds will stay with their hunted hare rather than switching to a fresh quarry if one is jumped during a hunt.

Scenting comes quite naturally to the Beagle. After all, following a scent trail is the primary purpose for which this breed has been developed through hundreds of years of selective breeding. When you take Bailey for a walk, you will notice his tendency to put his nose to the ground and explore the many fascinating scents. Any untrained hound will follow a trail when prompted by his own natural interest, but if you plan to participate in tracking with your Beagle, you will need to train him to work on command. It is also vital that you provide strong incentive and positive motivation for him to follow the designated trail.

Basic Tracking Equipment

Before you can begin Bailey's training for tracking work, you will need to obtain certain rather specific pieces of equipment:

Beagles are naturally expert trackers.

115

■ The harness must be comfortable, correctly fitted, and nonrestrictive. This important piece of equipment provides for direct contact between you and your Beagle while tracking. A tracking harness consists of one loop that slides over Bailey's head and a second loop that fits around his midsection. These two loops are connected by a top and bottom strap. There is no strap across the shoulders (as might be found on a draft-style harness) that would restrict free movement and apply pressure when your hound pulls against the harness during tracking.

■ A tracking line should be of sufficient length to put you far enough behind your Beagle to observe and read his body language while working. Some handlers prefer a 20-foot (6-m) leash, while others recommend 40 feet (12 m)

Tracking requires a variety of accessories.

of line be used at all times. Leashes made of 3/8-inch (9.5-mm) cotton webbing are popular, but almost anything will do, as long as it is easy to let out and take up when Bailey is moving away or toward you.

■ Stakes and flagging are used to mark the starting point and also the turns during early training. You can use wooden dowels cut to a length of about 3 to 4 feet (91–122 cm) and sharpened on one end. A half dozen or so flags should be a sufficient number to start with. To the top of each stake, glue or staple a piece of bright orange or pink surveyor's tape so that they will be easily visible at a distance. It is also recommended that you carry a roll or two of surveyor's tape with you into the tracking field. Pieces can be torn off and tied onto a bush, fence, or tuft of grass to indicate turns or other features.

■ A bag or jacket with a large pouch in the front will come in handy for carrying all of the supplies you will need during training or while working a track.

■ Scent articles might include such items as an old leather glove, well-worn shoe, or a handkerchief that has been carried in your pocket.

■ Additional items should include appropriate gear for the potential weather conditions, such as a raincoat and boots. Don't forget to also bring a bowl and fresh water for Bailey, and refreshments for yourself and the tracklayer as well. As training progresses, include a clipboard and supplies for the tracklayer to use when mapping out the more complex tracks.

Training and Incentive

You will find tracking to be a far more enjoyable pastime if you take the approach of using positive motivation. Beagles are rather independent thinkers, and Bailey is likely to perform better if he is motivated to *want* to find the glove at the end of the track. In contrast, if you try to *force* your hound to track, he is likely to lack the determination to do so under difficult conditions and neither one of you will have much fun.

There are numerous ways in which you can motivate Bailey. One technique involves taking him for a long, leisurely walk through the field after each training session. If you can trust him off leash, release him and encourage play. Practice informal *recalls* and reward with food and praise. If Bailey enjoys a game of *Fetch*, have him retrieve the glove or other scent articles for you. The point is to let your Beagle know that he gets to have fun and explore after he completes a track. It also allows him an opportunity to become familiar with the natural conditions and cover he is likely to encounter during a typical tracking test.

Other techniques include schooling multiple dogs at a time. Jealousy between them can be a powerful motivator to perform. Food, double-laid tracks, and shorter tracks interspersed with playtime can also help motivate a less-than-enthusiastic tracking Beagle. Whatever methods of motivation you use, keep in mind that creating incentive is only a tool; training should remain focused on teaching Bailey to follow the scent trail.

AKC Tracking Tests

Tracking tests are noncompetitive events in which your Beagle must demonstrate his willingness and ability to follow the scent trail of a person under a variety of conditions. He also needs to locate the item dropped by that person at the end of the track. You must follow behind the dog at a distance of not less than 20 feet (6 m). It is permissible to verbally encourage Bailey during the test, but you may not use any commands or signals that might indicate the location or direction of the track. It is up to the judges to determine if the performance of a handler and dog team merits the granting of a tracking title. While there is no time limit within which you and Bailey must complete a track, if he clearly quits working the trail, he will fail the test.

Following a scent was the original purpose of this breed.

Home Schooling

As with any form of training, you will do well to keep in mind Bailey's individual temperament and abilities. No single approach to tracking will be the best method for every dog. The following is meant as a general guide to aid you in getting started. If your goal is to become involved in tracking tests or actual search and rescue work, you should seek out the assistance of an experienced trainer or tracking club.

Starting Out

Before you can begin training Bailey to track, you will need to find an appropriate, available location. Seek out a level field of several acres covered in short grass or other low vegetation. Try to avoid areas of high use by humans or animals, or those littered with obsta-

The first step is glove work.

cles, as your hound does not need these sorts of distractions during early training. Your goal is to make this a fun activity for Bailey, while teaching the basic commands and behaviors. While it is not impossible to work solo, training sessions will be much more productive if two people are involved right from the start. This way, one person can act as the tracklayer, while the other handles the Beagle. The following exercises are presented with the assumption that both a tracklayer and separate handler (you) are involved in each training session.

Glove work. The first few days of training should be dedicated to motivating the Beagle to want to find the scent article, typically a glove, located at the end of a track. This method of training is commonly referred to as glove work. You will need to bring along two tracking stakes, a glove, tempting food rewards, and Bailey's tracking harness and leash.

1. Begin by kneeling next to Bailey and restraining him by the collar or harness so that he is not able to follow the tracklayer. The tracklayer then shows the hound the glove and lays it on the ground with a piece of food positioned on top.
2. Once Bailey is aware of the baited glove and demonstrates obvious interest, the tracklayer should back up several more steps before again placing the glove and food on the ground.

3. Allow your Beagle to immediately run to the glove and retrieve his treat while you praise him lavishly. The goal is for him to get excited about locating the glove, and anything else he associates with it.

While food is the strongest motivator for most Beagles, use whatever reward works best for Bailey. If a game of *Fetch*, a favorite toy, or the glove by itself interests your hound more than food, then use that instead. Repeat this glove work several times until your hound responds with consistent interest.

The First Track

Although Bailey will likely be finding the glove by sight at this point, and not by scent, the time has come to lay the first track. This initial track should be about 15 feet (4.5 m) in length; the length of the tracks can be gradually increased over several days and as Bailey's training progresses.

1. The tracklayer begins by walking a few paces away from you and your hound, with the glove and food in hand, and plants the first stake in the ground. He should then turn around and face the Beagle, drawing his attention to the fact that he is holding the glove and food item.

2. Once the hound shows an interest in the glove, the tracklayer turns and walks an additional 15 feet (4.5 m) away before planting the second tracking stake in the ground.

3. The tracklayer then turns and again shows the Beagle the glove and food while encouraging him to come and get it. Firmly restrain the hound from doing so, while the tracklayer places the glove and food on the ground, walks back to the starting stake (taking care to follow the same path), and quietly takes up a position behind the hound and you.

4. The Beagle is then told to *"Go find!"* and permitted to run to the glove for his reward, on leash and followed by you, the handler.

This type of track is known as a *double-laid track*, meaning that the tracklayer walks the same line twice. Double-laid tracks are often used during early training, until the hound becomes less dependent upon visual cues and learns to follow the scent trail when searching for the glove. During these early sessions, do not expect Bailey to use his nose extensively, though some hounds will automatically do so. As training progresses, and the tracks become more challenging, he will be more inclined to rely upon his nose to locate the trail and any articles hidden along the way. Keep sessions short, and praise and reward him each time he finds the article at the end of the track.

Subsequent Sessions

Continue to work with Bailey in this way at least once a week, although two or three outings a week would be

Home Schooling

better. Begin with basic glove work to motivate him, followed by several short, easy tracks. Steadily increase the length of the tracks, and if he remains enthusiastic about tracking, you can gradually phase out the glove work. When the track lengths reach about 50 yards (46 m), Bailey will probably no longer be able to find the glove by visual means alone. This is when he will naturally begin to use his nose to follow the track, if he hasn't done so already. If he wanders too far off of the trail while searching, gently guide him back and point out the location of the ground trail.

Once your Beagle is capably completing a straight track of approximately 30 to 50 yards (27–46 m) in length, it is time to introduce the single-laid track and turns. Begin to establish a routine of always placing

This Beagle has good contact with the track scent.

the tracking harness and long line onto him at the start of each training session and removing them when work is done. You should also consistently follow him at a distance of not less than 20 feet (6 m) while tracking, as is required during the AKC tracking test.

Single-Laid Tracks

To create a basic, single-laid track, the tracklayer should proceed just as he did when laying the 50-yard (46-m) double-laid tracks, right up to where he drops the glove next to the article flag. At this point, the tracklayer should continue walking straight ahead for a short distance before turning and quietly circling back around to a position behind the hound and you. The tracklayer must be careful to circle wide, a minimum of about 10 yards (9 m) away from the track and preferably downwind, so that the scent of his return path does not cause confusion. While the scent will be less concentrated on a single-laid track, this type of challenge should not be particularly difficult for your Beagle. When he seems to be comfortable with the single-laid tracks, throw in a turn.

Introducing Turns

When introducing turns in the track for the first time, try to do so on a still day so that the airborne scent does not create a confusing situation for your Beagle. Start out with just one turn on an

A flag marks the turn.

otherwise straight track. The tracklayer should place a flag at the turn, in addition to the flags at the start and finish of the track. Marking the turn will allow you to immediately identify any problems the hound is having and correct him.

This first turn should be an *open* turn, meaning it is less than 90 degrees from the original direction of the track. Initially, you might find it helpful to go back to following Bailey closer, perhaps using a 6-foot (1.8-m) leash, so that you can make corrections before he gets too far off the track. Go back to the regulation 20-foot (6-m) leash once he is working turns well without assistance. In subsequent training sessions, turns can be made that are closer to

90 degrees. Begin to vary the directions of the turns (right or left) and gradually add multiple turns within the same track, with legs of 30 to 50 yards (27–46 m) in between.

When your Beagle is working a marked track, make note of his demeanor. You will need to be able to "read" your dog and recognize his tracking behaviors for when you attempt to run *a blind track.* Watch how he behaves while working the track, and his reaction when he momentarily loses contact with the scent or is puzzling out a turn. All of this will be important in helping you to trust in him when you are faced with working an unmarked track, such as during a tracking test.

Following an intriguing scent.

Certification

Before being permitted to participate in an AKC tracking test, the Beagle must satisfactorily perform a certification test and be certified in writing by an approved or provisional tracking judge. This test shall be equivalent in complexity to the regular tracking test and administered under similar conditions. Once Bailey is certified, you will need to locate and enter licensed

tracking tests and hope for the best; due to the small number of tracks that can be completed in a day, a lottery system is used to determine which dog/handler teams will be invited to participate on any given test date. The Tracking Dog certificate will be issued, and the privilege of adding the TD suffix to Bailey's name permitted, when he has been certified by two judges as having passed a licensed or member club tracking test.

TDX and VST

The Tracking Dog Excellent test is used to demonstrate unquestionably that your Beagle has the ability to discriminate scent and the perseverance to do so under a wide variety of potentially difficult conditions. TDX tracks are longer and include more turns and obstacles. The purpose of the Variable Surface Tracking test is to verify the ability of your hound to recognize and follow a human scent while adapting to changing scenting conditions. Bailey must demonstrate a high level of motivation and persistence to earn his VST. A Champion Tracker Title certificate is issued to those dogs that earn all three tracking titles (TD, TDX, and VST), and the prefix of CT may be added to the name to signify they are Tracking Champions.

14 Agility

The Agile Beagle

What more appealing activity for an energetic hound and his owner could there possibly be than Agility? Imagine Bailey's enthusiasm as he climbs the A-frame, leaps over obstacles, and runs through a tunnel. Short of chasing rabbits through field and forest, you are unlikely to find a more entertaining or mutually enjoyable outlet for the pent-up energies of an athletic Beagle.

Canine Agility is a sport in which you must guide your Beagle, off leash, through a timed obstacle course. Participation in Agility provides a fun means of physical exercise and mental stimulation, while further strengthening the bond between hound and handler. Loosely modeled after equestrian stadium jumping, Agility has grown into a unique sport involving a variety of obstacles. In competitive Agility, you and your Beagle will be scored based on performance and the amount of time required to complete the course. Many people enjoy an informal involvement in Agility, just for the thrill of watching their dog navigate the obstacles and for its confidence-building qualities. Agility training is also frequently used as a tool to relieve the dog's boredom and increase his focus.

A Brief History

The idea of holding dog Agility demonstrations was first suggested in the late 1970s, when the Crufts Dog Show in Great Britain was searching for a means of entertaining spectators in the main arena area between completion of the Obedience championships and the start of group conformation judging. Agility made its debut as a spectator sport in 1979, and has continued to grow by leaps and bounds throughout Britain, Western Europe, and the Americas.

In the United States, there are numerous national organizations that sanction Agility trials and award titles. Most Agility events focus on the physical ability, accuracy, and speed with which the dogs maneuver the course, but some require less physical prowess, using lower jumps and simpler obstacles, focusing more on the handling aspects of the sport. This allows handlers and hounds of all ability levels the opportunity to participate in the fun of Agility.

As of August 1994 the American Kennel Club has offered licensed Agility competitions. During the first year, there were 23 AKC Agility trials in the United States. By 1998 interest had expanded to the point that more than 500 AKC trials were held throughout the country.

Pictured is the open tunnel.

Warning: Your Beagle's safety should always come first when participating in Agility. Young hounds should never be forced to jump or perform other strenuous activities. Landing on immature forelegs and shoulders can cause repeated trauma. This may result in injury with the potential for long-term disabilities. Likewise, your Beagle should be taught not to rush through the obstacles; a more controlled approach will help avoid accidents. If constructing your own practice obstacles, be sure they are sturdy and safe. Ramps should have cross-laths, and contact zones should have rough surfaces to provide for adequate traction.

Agility Trials and Titles

Agility courses are comprised of a specific group of obstacles that Bailey must negotiate correctly. Each course is timed, and the dog/handler team that finishes with the fewest course faults and the fastest time wins. You will be permitted to offer your Beagle an unlimited number of commands or signals, but may not touch either the equipment or your hound. Faults are given for actions such as knocking down a jump bar, failing to hit the contact zone while ascending or descending contact equipment, and taking obstacles out of sequence. In addition, time penalties are assessed against any team that exceeds the SCT (set course time).

Classes and Titles

The three basic levels of Agility competition are Novice, Open, and Agility Excellent. Within each class, there are five different jump height divisions to accommodate dogs of varying sizes. The titles earned include Novice Agility (NA), Open Agility (OA), and Agility Excellent (AX). The dog may acquire these titles by earning three *qualifying scores* in the corresponding classes on three separate occasions and under a minimum of two different judges.

The Master Agility Excellent (MX) title may be acquired after your Beagle has completed his AX requirements and continues on to earn qualifying scores in the Agility Excellent class at an additional ten licensed or member Agility trials. Within the past few years, further AKC Agility titles have been designed to recognize those dogs that exhibit superior performance in this sport. AKC Agility now also includes special Agility Jumpers with Weaves classes and titles (NAJ through MXJ). In these classes, participants are not slowed down by the careful performance and control required when facing the contact obstacles and pause table. This allows experienced competitors the opportunity to race through a course composed primarily of jumps, thereby demonstrating their dogs' speed and jumping ability. The Master Agility Championship (MACH) title is available to those dogs receiving a minimum of 750 championship points and 20 Double Qualifying scores in the Excellent B class, as defined in the AKC Regulations for Agility Trials.

The pause table is used to demonstrate control.

The Obstacles

Spectator appeal and the safety of participants were both considered when designing the standard Agility obstacles. To aid in the prevention of injuries, all jumps are designed with easily displaceable bars. The contact obstacles, those that your hound is required to physically scale, each have roughened surfaces that provide for ample traction. Because Bailey must touch the contact zones at the approach and exit of an obstacle with one or more paws or be faulted, the contact obstacles also enforce a careful, controlled approach to completing the Agility course.

During competition, the obstacles may be arranged in various course configurations, with the layout of the courses being unique from trial to trial. Courses are designed to offer different levels of challenges appropriate to the specific class and size division of dogs competing. You will be required to direct your Beagle through the obstacle course following a sequence that has been predetermined by the judge.

Contact obstacles. These include the dog walk, A-frame, and seesaw, and are usually made of wood. Bailey must climb over these obstacles, making sure to touch the yellow painted contact zones at the approach and exit of each one. The seesaw, or teeter, is a moving contact board, similar to the child's playground equipment of the same name.

Navigating the weave poles.

Tunnels. Two types of tunnels are used on an Agility course. The Open tunnels are relatively rigid and can be bent into various shapes for the dog to run through. The Chute, or Closed/Collapsed tunnel is made up of two parts. The entry portion is made of a rigid barrel onto which a chute of collapsible material has been attached. Your Beagle must enter the open end of the tunnel and then push his way through the chute material to emerge on the other side. While this can take longer for some hounds to master, the tunnels usually become a favorite obstacle and are a real crowd pleaser too.

Weave poles. These are a series of upright poles that the dog must navigate, weaving in and out until he reaches the end. He should enter with the first pole at his left shoulder and then proceed down the line. The number of poles can vary, with 6 to 12 being typical.

The pause table. This is used to demonstrate that your Beagle remains

Shown is the suspended hoop jump.

under control. Here he will stop and relax for a few seconds before continuing his run. The top is a 3 feet × 3 feet (91 × 91 cm) square and sits on a stand that is adjusted to accommodate the various height divisions. Dogs pause on this table for a count of five seconds before proceeding on to the next obstacle.

Jumps. These may include winged or wingless single hurdles, and a panel or wall jump. Agility courses also typically include a suspended tire, hoop, or window jump. The spread or oxer jumps may include the double bar, triple bar, and broad jump. There are additional specialized jumps, such as the water jumps and brush jumps, that might also be seen on an Agility course depending on the class and the sanctioning organization.

Preparing for Competition

Certainly it is possible to construct many of the basic obstacles at home in order to introduce your Beagle to this entertaining sport, but if competitive Agility and earning titles is your goal, there comes a time when home schooling will not suffice. At an Agility trial, Bailey must respond to your direction and complete the obstacles in sequence in front of a potentially distracting audience. In order to best prepare, it is highly recommended that you enroll in an Agility class. Classes are frequently sponsored by both Agility and Obedience training clubs. Contact information for the AKC and other Agility organizations is included in Useful Addresses and Literature beginning on page 143.

Home Schooling

Introducing the Obstacles

"Food treats are used to encourage the hound to approach a new piece of equipment. This is where the Beagle excels. Most Beagles will follow the treat through, over, or under any obstacle with a little encouragement. Start the training with all the equipment at their lowest position. This allows your hound to build his confidence. As he learns to maneuver his way through each obstacle, the trainer can increase the height, length, or angle of each piece of equipment. Praise generously and make it FUN!

"Always tell your Beagle the name of the specific obstacle as he approaches it. In time he will actually look for the obstacle when the handler mentions it by name. Use one-word names and be consistent. Use a hand signal to emphasize the direction the hound is to take and which obstacle he should negotiate next.

"Keep the sessions short. Introduce one new obstacle at a time. Start with one and every few days introduce another new obstacle. Mix up the order of obstacles to keep the hound paying attention and learning the names of the equipment. Always use praise—no negative commands. This should be fun! If your Beagle feels he is having fun, he will respond to the commands more quickly and a successful run will be completed."

—*Marie Morris*

The seesaw is a moving contact obstacle.

15 Conformation Shows

Showing dogs is a wonderful sport, where the thrill of competition is combined with the pleasure of seeing fine specimens of the various breeds. At a dog show, the main consideration is the hound's *conformation* or overall appearance, physical structure, and temperament. Your Beagle will be examined by a judge and then placed according to how closely (in the judge's opinion, and in comparison to the other entries) he measures up to the breed standard.

A show prospect puppy should have good angulation and balance.

The primary purpose of conformation shows is as a showcase for breeding stock. To be eligible for entry, Bailey must be AKC registered, at least six months old on the day of the show, and of a breed for which classes are offered in the premium list. Hounds that have been spayed or neutered are not eligible to compete in the regular classes, but may be exhibited in stud dog and brood bitch classes, if offered. Beagles with disqualifying faults, such as exceeding 15 inches (38 cm) in height, are ineligible for conformation competition. Most dog shows also include classes for Junior Showmanship.

Selecting a Show Prospect

If you intend to succeed at the shows, you must start with a good Beagle. Unless he is a quality representative of the breed, with sound structure, correct type, and level temperament, no amount of training is going to transform Bailey into a conformation show winner—so let's begin by considering what you should look for when choosing a promising show/breeding-prospect puppy.

You would do well to take into consideration all of the points previously mentioned in Chapter 3 regarding selection of a new Beagle companion, particularly those relating to temperament. A pleasant, outgoing, confident personality is doubly important in the future show puppy. When evaluating a potential show prospect, points relating to conformation, movement, and overall balance must also be considered. Try to arrange to examine the litter and make your selection at between eight and ten weeks of age. Be sure to familiarize yourself with the Beagle standard in advance, and don't be shy about taking a copy of the standard (or this book) with you to refer to as you examine each puppy.

Look for overall balance. A *four-square*, well-proportioned puppy with moderate angulation in shoulder and knee is highly desirable. *Built four square* implies that the hound's height, when measured from the ground to the top of the shoulder blade, should be equal to his length, when measured from the top of the tip of the shoulder blade to the back of the base of the tail. While they may be a bit stockier in appearance, eight-to-ten-week-old puppies should closely resemble an adult Beagle in basic structure and conformation.

Movement. At eight to ten weeks this can still be rather tricky to evaluate. Remember that good movement is directly related to correct structure, so if the puppy is built correctly, his movement should eventually pull together as well. Young pups rarely have the muscle devel-

opment to cope with their abundance of heavy bone, and this may result in some rather sloppy movement. Look for the puppy that occasionally gaits cleanly, without much crossing and weaving. Front legs should swing almost straight forward, without twisting out at the elbows or toeing in. Rears should not move too close, and twisting of the hocks should be minimal.

Free stacking. Those pups possessing the best conformation and balance will tend to *free-stack* themselves when they pause, with every foot falling perfectly into place. Correct toplines remain level whether the puppy is running with his nose to the ground or head held high. Each Beagle's personality and attitude are also evident as they interact with one another. A hound with an outgoing, fearless nature is preferable for exhibition purposes. Often, the more dominant puppies will possess more of that priceless "look at me" attitude that is invaluable in a good show dog.

The Beagle Breed Standard

The Beagle standard is a written description of the ideal physical specimen. It is a carefully laid-out blueprint, specifying those characteristics that would allow the Beagle to best function afield with efficiency and a minimum of fatigue. Included are additional traits regarding distinguishing breed type.

The first Beagle standard written in this country was approved by the American

English Beagle Club in 1884. Compiled by a committee consisting of General Richard Rowett, Dr. H. L. Twaddell, and Norman Elmore, this standard was written as a description of the general's fine, dual-purpose Beagles and actually differed very little from the English standard. Today's current AKC Beagle standard has changed very little over the years.

Current, Official AKC Breed Standard for the Beagle

(Approved on September 10, 1957)

Head

The skull should be fairly long, slightly domed at occiput, with cranium broad and full.

Ears: Ears set on moderately low, long, reaching when drawn out nearly if not quite to the end of the nose; fine in texture, fairly broad—with almost entire absence of erectile power—setting close to the head, with the forward edge slightly inturning to the cheek—rounded at tip.

Eyes: Eyes large, set well apart—soft and houndlike—expression gentle and pleading; of a brown or hazel color.

Muzzle: Muzzle of medium length—straight and square-cut—the stop moderately defined.

Jaws: Level. Lips free from flews; nostrils large and open.

This is a correct head with soft expression.

Defects: A very flat skull, narrow across the top; excess of dome, eyes small, sharp and terrierlike, or prominent and protruding; muzzle long, snipy or cut away decidedly below the eyes, or very short. Roman-nosed or upturned giving a dish-faced expression. Ears short, set on high or with a tendency to rise above the point of origin.

Body

Neck and Throat: Neck rising free and light from the shoulders strong in substance yet not loaded, of medium length. A slight wrinkle below the angle of the jaw, however, may be allowable. **Defects:** A thick, short, cloddy neck carried on a line with the top of the shoulders. Throat showing dewlap and folds of skin to a degree termed "throatiness."

Shoulders and Chest: Shoulders sloping—clean, muscular, not heavy or loaded—conveying the idea of freedom of action with activity and strength. Chest deep and broad, but not broad enough to interfere with the free play of the shoulders. **Defects:** Straight, upright shoulders. Chest disproportionately wide or with lack of depth.

Back, Loin and Ribs: Back short, muscular and strong. Loin broad and slightly arched, and the ribs well sprung, giving abundance of lung room. **Defects:** very long or swayed or roached back. Flat, narrow loin, flat ribs.

Forelegs and Feet

Forelegs: Straight with plenty of bone in proportion to size of the hound. Pasterns short and straight.

The black, tan, and white tricolor is a common hound color.

Feet: Close, round and firm. Pad full and hard. **Defects:** Out at elbows. Knees knuckled over forward, or bent backward. Forelegs crooked or Dachshundlike. Feet long, open or spreading.

Hips, Thighs, Hind Legs and Feet: Hips and thighs strong and well muscled, giving abundance of propelling power. Stifles strong and well let down. Hocks firm, symmetrical and moderately bent. Feet close and firm. **Defects:** Cowhocks, or straight hocks. Lack of muscle and propelling power. Open feet.

Tail

Set moderately high; carried gaily, but not turned forward over the back with slight curve; short as compared with size of the hound; with brush. **Defects:** A long tail. Teapot curve or inclined forward from the root. Rat tail with absence of brush.

Coat

A close, hard, hound coat of medium length. **Defects:** A short, thin coat or of a soft quality.

Color

Any true hound color.

General Appearance

A miniature Foxhound, solid and big for his inches, with the wear-and-tear look of a hound that can last in the chase and follow his quarry to the death.

Scale of Points

Head

Skull	5	
Ears	10	
Eyes	5	
Muzzle	5	25

Body

Neck	5	
Chest and Shoulders	15	
Back, Loin and Ribs	15	35

Running Gear

Forelegs	10	
Hips, Thighs and Hind Legs	10	
Feet	10	30

Coat	5	
Stern	5	10
TOTAL		100

Varieties

There shall be two varieties:

Thirteen Inch—which shall be for hounds not exceeding 13 inches in height.

Fifteen Inch—which shall be for hounds over 13 but not exceeding 15 inches in height.

Disqualification

Any hound measuring more than 15 inches shall be disqualified.

The standard includes further points relating to the judging of organized Beagle packs, omitted here due to space limitations. The complete breed standard may be viewed on the AKC web site. (Reprinted with the permission of the National Beagle Club of America.)

A Brief Discussion of the Standard

Paget (1923) remarks that "the man who keeps hounds for hunting may be trusted to breed the sort most suitable for their purpose." In general, form should (and typically does) follow function. The Beagle we see today is the result of hundreds of years of selective breeding for an efficient little hunting hound, built for endurance to follow his quarry to the end.

Height is currently the only breed-specific disqualification in Beagles. In the United States, 15 inches (38 cm) is the limit, while in Great Britain (and most other countries) 16 inches (41 cm) is the maximum desired height at the withers. Beagle height is measured at the highest point of the shoulder blade (the withers) using a wicket.

Although the AKC Beagle standard fails to mention movement, this is clearly an important point to be considered when evaluating these active little scent-hounds. Movement reflects structure, and the correctly built Beagle should move smoothly, with no wasted motion, covering ground efficiently and with purpose.

Preparation for the Show Ring

Most hounds do not naturally enjoy trotting around the ring with their nose well off the ground, and standing politely while a judge performs a rather personal, hands-on examination. Your Beagle will require proper training, grooming, and conditioning to succeed in the show ring. He must learn to love the attention and to show himself with enthusiasm—and you will need to learn how to present him to his best advantage. Dog shows are the one sport where you, as an amateur owner, can step into the ring and compete head to head with the professionals. While that may seem a bit intimidating at first, owner/handlers can and often do beat the pros on a regular basis.

Training your Beagle to show is very similar to the way you taught basic obedience. You will use a system of rewards and praise for desirable behavior, and ignore or redirect inappropriate behavior. You want Bailey to learn to love everything about showing so that he presents an upbeat and enthusiastic picture in the ring. Keep sessions short and try to remain focused on making show training fun rather than demanding perfect behavior.

Show training consists of teaching two basic behaviors: *stacking* (standing for examination) and *gaiting*. These two elements should be taught during separate sessions until your Beagle thoroughly understands both concepts. The transition between standing calmly, gaiting enthusiastically, and then settling back into a calm stack is difficult for a young hound to master.

Stack Training

Stack training should be started as soon as you get your new puppy. Ideally, Bailey should become accustomed to being handled and placed into a show stack, on a raised table, by 12 weeks of age. He must learn to accept examination of his mouth and head, and to permit judges to run their hands over his entire body. It is wise to at least initially practice stacking in front of a mirror, so that you can see how your Beagle will look from the judge's side.

If Bailey fidgets, constantly moving his feet out of position, you will need to get a firmer grip on his head. Grasp him under his chin, with your bent fingers fitting into the lower jaw while you firmly grip his right lip under your thumb. For those hounds that toss their head loose, try wrapping your thumb up and over the top of the muzzle to maintain control. This may not be comfortable for Bailey, but eventually he will figure out that struggling is futile and it is better to cooperate and stand still.

Once you have worked out the most effective method of stacking your Beagle, with all four feet placed correctly, stick with it. In the ring, you will want to be able to stack your hound as quickly and consistently as possible in a position that makes him look good. As you and your Beagle gain experience, it may be helpful to get into a stacking routine of positioning the feet, pulling down the lip on the judge's side, smoothing back the ear set, smoothing the topline, and finally lifting the tail into a proud position. The hound thus presented creates a nice image when the judge turns to look at your Beagle.

Gaiting

Gaiting on a loose lead should be taught during this same time frame, although in separate sessions. Actually, I have found it simpler to teach my show-prospect puppies to walk along at my left side off leash first, and then introduce the show leash later. The important thing to remember when breaking a Beagle to leash is to never issue harsh corrections, jerking or dragging the puppy along. Always use positive motivation and reinforcement to encourage your hound into position. You want him to step out gaily and love to show. Jerking the leash to try and force a lagging hound into position only results in his dragging his feet more. Bribe him with a little bait or a favorite squeaky toy instead. Once he is trotting along nicely and paying attention, praise and reward lavishly.

Only after Bailey has mastered the separate lessons of stacking and gaiting should you attempt to combine the two. With practice, he will slowly learn how to make a smooth transition from standing

The tail should be carried gaily when gaiting.

quietly to moving and back to standing again. Build gradually, and try not to expect too much of your young Beagle. Keep it fun, especially the first few times out in public, either at training classes or a show. Forget about winning or losing and make it an enjoyable experience for your puppy. As he matures further, both mentally and physically, the polite behavior and wins will come on their own, without rushing him. Don't crush the spirit of your exuberant young hound in the desire for a perfect performance. It is far better to progress gradually, and have a hound that will show with consistent enthusiasm over the long haul.

Note: During training you will also be watching and learning about your Beagle. What does he like and dislike? How does he respond to different situations or stimuli? Knowing what turns your hound on and what calms him down will come in handy in the show ring. As an owner/handler this is one area where you have a distinct advantage over the professional. Because you live with Bailey, you can observe him on a daily basis and learn how to most effectively motivate him to put in the best possible performance.

Handling Classes

Show handling classes are sponsored by many of the all-breed kennel clubs. These classes provide an opportunity for you, as a novice handler, to learn how to present your dog while becoming familiar with typical show ring procedures. Classes are not, however, the best way to prepare your new puppy for the ring. Most of Bailey's show training should take place at home, where sessions can be kept short and there are fewer distractions. The problem with trying to teach a puppy show ring behaviors in a class setting is that classes are typically an hour long. Not only will you never spend a full hour actually competing, nonstop, in the show ring with your Beagle, but such a lengthy session is likely to result in a bored or exhausted puppy. Socialization with other dogs and people is important, but can be accomplished instead by attending puppy

This is a neatly groomed and presented Beagle.

kindergarten, or by simply taking Bailey out in public on a regular basis.

You will benefit far more from show classes if you are able to borrow a mature, trained dog from a friend and then use the classes to work on your own handling skills. If that is not an option, then wait until Bailey has at least mastered the basics of stacking and gaiting at home before enrolling in a handling class. Attend classes with the goal of keeping it fun for your hound. It is important for you to learn how to best present your Beagle in the ring, but in doing so you do not want to destroy his spirit and enthusiasm.

Match Shows

There are several types of dog shows, including those in which the dogs are competing for points toward their championship titles, and those designed primarily for practice. These practice shows are called *match shows* or *puppy matches*. They may be held for fun, or AKC sanctioned and held following AKC rules and procedures. At a match show, the sponsoring club members are often learning how to organize and run this type of event. The judges and ring stewards may also be practicing their rolls. And matches are the perfect place for novice handlers and inexperienced dogs to learn and practice the show ring routine. No championship points are awarded at match shows, and the entire event is a bit more relaxed and friendly than the highly competitive point shows.

Bailey's first exposure to shows should be in a puppy match. Groom him and come prepared, just as if this is an important show—but remember that your focus should not be on trying to win. Wins at a match show may be fun, but they mean very little. You are here instead to learn and become comfortable with show ring procedure. Most important, you are here to teach Bailey to enjoy the shows. Walk him around the show site and allow him to adjust to the many new and exciting sights, sounds, and smells. Permit people to pet him and make a fuss over your cute Beagle puppy. Encourage him to stand for examination and then praise and give him a treat for his good behavior. Better yet, hand a treat to the other person and let him or her give it to your hound. In this way he learns that allowing a stranger to examine him is a rewarding experience.

Conditioning and Grooming

You will of course want to present Bailey in his best possible condition for the judge's consideration. Be sure to provide proper amounts of food and exercise so that your Beagle will not be too fat or overly thin, and to provide for adequate muscle development. Remember that the breed standard calls for the look of "a hound that can last in the chase." This means that the Beagle should appear to be in fit working condition, regardless of whether or not you actually hunt with him.

Grooming for the show ring involves more than just routine brushing and an occasional bath.

■ Neatening of the coat includes trimming and shaping to produce the most flattering outline and clean appearance.

■ A good pair of thinning shears is used to remove excess coat from under the neck and around the hindquarters.

■ Curved shears are helpful for shaping the tail tip and the *pants* on the back of the thighs.

■ Removal of whiskers is optional, as these are important sensory organs for the hunting hound.

■ Clippers are frequently used to clean up the stray hairs from under the belly, on the inner thighs, and occasionally on the underside of the neck and ears as well.

Correct grooming practices are best learned from more experienced exhibitors. It is a wise investment to offer to pay a professional Beagle handler or successful owner/handler to demonstrate to you the best way to groom your individual hound. Because the trimmed coat takes some time to blend in and begin to look natural, initial trimming and shaping should be done a month or two in advance of Bailey's first show. Repeated grooming and touch-up trimming, spread out over several weeks' time, will result in a neater-looking coat and outline.

The Classes

At the AKC shows, there are six regular classes in which dogs seeking points may compete. These classes include Puppy (may be subdivided into 6 to 9 Months and 9 to 12 Months), 12 to 18 Months, Novice, Bred by Exhibitor, American Bred, and Open. All dogs must be a minimum of

Show prospect puppies require an outgoing temperament.

six months old on or before the date of the show in order to be eligible for entry in an AKC point show.

Regular Classes

The Beagles competing in the regular classes are commonly referred to as *class dogs*. During the regular classes, there is no intersex competition. The males compete only against other males, and the females against other females. Only one male (dog) and one female (bitch) of each size variety will be awarded championship points at each show. The judging proceeds as a process of elimination; only the first-place winner of each class remains in competition.

Winners Class

After the judge has finished evaluating all of the male class entries, the undefeated, first-place winners from each class are brought back to compete against one another. This is the Winners class. The judge selects what he feels is the best dog from among these class winners to be named Winners Dog, this is the dog that will receive championship points for the day. Next, the dog that placed second to the Winners Dog in his original class is brought into the ring to compete with the remaining class winners for Reserve Winners Dog. The Reserve Winners Dog will receive points only if for some reason the Winners Dog is later disqualified. The same process is repeated among the female class entries, resulting in a Winners Bitch (the only female in the variety to receive points at the show) and a Reserve Winners Bitch.

Best of Breed/ Variety Class

Finally, the Best of Breed/Variety class is judged. Champions of record, and those hounds that recently completed the requirements for championship according to their owners, may be entered for BOV competition. The Winners Dog and Winners Bitch also must continue on to compete for Best of Variety. The judge will examine each of the Champions (also called *specials*) and review the Winners, selecting one hound as the Best of Variety. Then, between the Winners Dog and Winners Bitch, the judge selects a Best of

Winners. The judge completes variety judging by selecting a Best of Opposite Sex to the Best of Variety.

In Beagles, the two size varieties are judged separately. This entire process occurs independently for the under 13-inch (33-cm) variety Beagles, and for those over 13 inches but not exceeding 15 inches (38 cm) in height. The Best of Variety winners representing the two sizes of Beagles do not compete for an ultimate Best of Breed award, except at independently held specialty shows. At the AKC all-breed shows, the two varieties are both represented in the hound group, and no intervariety competition is permitted at the breed level.

Junior Showmanship

In addition to the competitions taking place in the conformation ring, many kennel clubs offer classes for Junior Showmanship. Here the focus falls not on the quality of the dog but instead on the abilities and performance of the young handler. The AKC Junior Showmanship program offers participants the opportunity to develop their handling skills while learning about dog events and sportsmanship in general.

AKC Junior Showmanship classes are open to young people ranging in age from 10 to 18 years. Prospective junior handlers can best learn what is involved by watching the Junior Showmanship classes at a dog show. All participants in Junior Showmanship classes must obtain an AKC Junior Showmanship Handler

Number. You can apply for a number and obtain a copy of the *Rules and Regulations for Junior Showmanship* by contacting the American Kennel Club at the address provided on page 143.

Earning Championship and Beyond

The majority of dogs attending a show are competing for points toward their Championship. In order for Bailey to become an AKC Champion of record, he must earn a total of 15 points. These points must include at least two major wins under different judges, and also one or more points won under a third judge. Points are awarded based on the number of eligible

CH. LANBUR MISS FLEETWOOD—the top winning Beagle in American history.

dogs in actual competition. Each year, the AKC compiles a schedule of points for each gender within each breed/variety, further divided by geographical location. This schedule is used to equalize the relative difficulty of obtaining points, a major win, and Championship.

Attaining his Championship does not necessarily need be the conclusion of Bailey's show career. Many dogs continue to compete at the Best of Variety level and beyond, because their owners believe in their animal's superior quality. If Bailey is a fine example of the breed, and you both enjoy the excitement of the show ring, then you may decide to continue on and make BOV, Group level, or Best in Show wins your ultimate goal.

Attending Your First Point Show

As a Spectator

Attending a dog show as a spectator is an important first step in learning about this sport. Local dog shows are often advertised in the newspaper and on television. You can also find information on upcoming shows through the Internet, either on the AKC web site or sites belonging to the various dog show superintendents (such as *www.infodog.com*). Through the superintendent or host club, you should be able to obtain information regarding the time and ring location where Beagles will be judged. Be sure to purchase a copy of the show catalog, which contains information

pertaining to all of the dogs entered in the show, and contact information for their owners. The catalog will tell you which hounds are entered in which classes, and can aid you in following the progression of judging.

Additional tips for first time dog show spectators include:
- Plan to arrive early. Once a breed has been judged, those dogs are usually permitted to leave. Arrive too late, and you'll miss the opportunity to see them.
- Never attempt to pet a dog without asking permission first; the dog may have just been groomed in preparation for competition. Also, some dogs may enjoy attention and petting, while others may not be as trustworthy with strangers.
- Do seek out and talk to breeders and handlers; they can help to answer your questions about the judging, and conformation Beagles in particular. But as a courtesy, always wait until after they have finished exhibiting their hounds and are not too busy to talk.
- No matter how tempting, leave your own Beagle at home! You are here to observe and learn, not to show off your cute puppy. Most clubs have restrictions against unentered dogs being brought onto the show grounds anyway.

As an Exhibitor

Your first point show with Bailey should come only after you have competed in several match shows and are confident in his performance. Hopefully, you are also becoming confident in your abilities as a handler and feel relatively at ease with the normal ring procedure. A positive attitude will travel right down the leash to your dog. Likewise, if you are nervous, Bailey will sense your uneasiness.

1. **Arrive Early.** You need to have plenty of time and should not feel rushed. Allow your Beagle to relax in a comfortable location until closer to your scheduled ring time. Take a chair and position yourself outside your assigned ring. Watch your judge evaluating a few classes, so that you will know where to stand and what gaiting patterns he or she is using that day. While you are at ringside, approach the steward and ask to pick up your numbered armband. Double-check to see if the judging is running on schedule, so that you know how much time you have before your class is called. As your ring time approaches, take Bailey for a leisurely walk to relieve himself, and then do a little last-minute brushing and grooming. Brushing your hound can help both of you to relax and become mentally focused prior to competition.

2. **Come Prepared for Both Your Beagle's Needs and Your Own.** Don't forget to bring bowls and water from home, grooming supplies, the proper show leashes, and bait. Also bring along a folding chair and refreshments for yourself; these items may or may not be available at the show site. Bring along your entry confirmation that you should have received in the mail about a week in advance. Check the show catalog to make sure that there are no errors in your entry information. If there are, the superintendent will need

to be notified so that they can make a correction in the judge's book.

3. **Pay Close Attention During Judging.** Don't allow yourself to become involved in ringside chatter and lose track of what is happening in the ring—you could miss your class completely! When the steward calls for you to enter the ring, do so promptly. Calmly stack Bailey in the location specified and then listen for the judge's directions. At this first show, you want to concentrate on presenting your Beagle properly. Try to keep it enjoyable for Bailey, but at the same time never lose your focus. When your class is over, remain at ringside until your variety judging has been completed. If Bailey won his class, you will need to go back in to compete for Winners. If he took second, you may still need to go back in for Reserve, should the first-place hound from your class be awarded WD.

4. **Always Be a Gracious Winner—or Loser.** When you win, be courteous and move away from the ring entrance before celebrating with your friends. When someone else wins, congratulate the winners and then accept your lower placement ribbon with a polite "Thank you" to the judge, even if you are a little disappointed. Display good sportsmanship both in and out of the ring. When Bailey loses, it may be because he did not show well on that day, or your presentation left something to be desired, or perhaps his competition was simply the better specimen. Try to make each show a learning experience, so that you can better present Bailey the next time around.

Useful Addresses and Literature

Breed Books

Black, Glenn "Old Kickapoo." *American Beagling*. New York: G. P. Putnam's Sons, 1949.

Bryden, H. A. *Hare Hunting and Harriers*. London: Grant Richards, 1903.

Carrel, Ike W. *The Beagle Standard with Interpretations*. 1929.

Denlinger, William. *The Complete Beagle*. Richmond, VA: Denlinger's, 1956.

Foy, Marcia, and Anna Katherine Nicholas. *The Beagle*. Neptune City, NJ: T.F.H. Publications, 1985.

Musladin, Judith and Anton, and Ada Lueke. *The New Beagle*. New York: Howell Book House, 1998.

Nicholas, Anna Katherine, and Joan McDonald Brearley. *The Wonderful World of Beagles and Beagling*. Neptune City, NJ: T.F.H. Publications, 1975.

Paget, J. Otho. *Beagles and Beagling*. London: Hutchinson and Co., 1923.

Prentice, H. W. *The Beagle in America and England*. DeKalb, IL: H. W. Prentice and W. A. Powel, 1920.

Training Books

Alston, George, and Connie Vanacore. *The Winning Edge; Show Ring Secrets*. New York: Howell Book House, 1992.

American Kennel Club. *American Kennel Club Dog Care and Training*. New York: Howell Book House, 1991.

Davis, L. Wilson. *Go Find! Training Your Dog to Track*. New York: Howell Book House, 1974.

Saunders, Blaunche. *The Complete Book of Dog Obedience*. New York: Howell Book House, 1978.

Simmons-Moake, Jane. *Agility Training*. New York: Howell Book House, 1991.

Periodicals and Newsletters

NBC Supporting Membership Newsletter
622 Mistflower Drive
Acworth, GA 30102

Hounds and Hunting Magazine
P.O. Box 372
554 Derrick Road
Bradford, PA 16701

Better Beagling
P.O. Box 8142
Essex, VT 05451

The Rabbit Hunter
c/o Gerald Bailey
P.O. Box 557
Royston, GA 30662

The Beagle Annual
Hoflin Publishing
4401 Zephyr Street
Wheat Ridge, CO 80033-3299

Show Beagle Quarterly
378 Tyler Road NW
Albuquerque, NM 87107

The AKC Gazette
P.O. Box 1956
Marion, OH 43306
(800) 533-7323

Organizations

American Kennel Club (AKC)
5580 Centerview Drive, Suite 200
Raleigh, NC 27606-3390
(919) 233-9767
Fax: (919) 233-3627
Web site: *www.akc.org*

United Kennel Club (UKC)
100 East Kilgore Road
Kalamazoo, MI 49002-5584
(616) 343-9020
Fax: (616) 343-7037
Web site: *www.ukcdogs.com*

Canadian Kennel Club
89 Skyway Avenue, Suite 100
Etobicoke, Ontario
Canada M9W 6R4
(416) 675-5511
Fax: (416) 675-6506
Web site: *www.ckc.ca*

Breed Associations

National Beagle Club of America
Institute Farm
22265 Oatlands Road
Aldie, VA 20105
Web site: *clubs.akc.org/NBC/*

NBC Supporting Membership Secretary
Mrs. Nadine Chicoine
P.O. Box 1710
Leonardtown, MD 20650

American Rabbit Hound Association
   (ARHA)
P.O. Box 557
Royston, GA 30662-0557
(706) 245-0081
Fax: (706) 245-0076
Web site: *www.arha.com*

Rescue

Beagle Rescue Foundation of America
National Headquarters
148 Park Lane
Middle Island, NY 11953
Web site: *brfoa.tripod.com*

Activities

Therapy Dogs International, Inc.
88 Bartley Rd.
Flanders, NJ 07836
(973) 252-9800
Web site: *www.tdi-dog.org*

Delta Society
289 Perimeter Rd. E.
Renton, WA 98055-1329
(206) 226-1329
Web site: *www.petsforum.com/
   deltasociety/dsj000.htm*

United States Dog Agility Association
   (USDAA)
P.O. Box 850955
Richardson, TX 75085-0995
(214) 231-9700
Web site: *www.usdaa.com*

North American Dog Agility Council, Inc.
   (NADAC)
HCR 2, Box 277
St. Maries, ID 83861
Web site: *www.nadac.com*

Web Sites

The Beagle Network: *dogjunction.com/
   beagle/*
The Regal Beagle: *members.aol.com/
   cokicola/beagle.htm*
Beagles on the Web: *www.beagles-on-
   the-web.com*
Beagle Rescue Page: *www.beagles-on-the-
   web.com/adopt/*
Beagle Resource Center:
   members.tripod.com/beagle_resources/
Beagle Information Site: *www.beagleinfo.
   com*
Beagle Breed FAQ's: *www.geocities.com/
   brbeagles/beaglefaq.html*
Drs. Foster and Smith's Pet Education
   Center: *www.peteducation.com*
The Dog Obedience and Training Page:
   www.dogpatch.org/obed/
The Dog Agility Page: *www.dogpatch.org/
   agility/*
INFODOG: *www.infodog.com*

Safe chew items provide entertainment.

Glossary

Activity training: Training for specialized activities, such as hunting, field trial competition, or Agility.

Airborne scent: Body scent of an animal that is carried upwards by air currents.

AKC: The American Kennel Club; largest registry of purebred dogs in the United States.

Alpha: The pack leader, or dominant individual, in the social hierarchy of the household.

Angulation: Term used to refer to the slant of the bones and the size of the resulting angles, mainly in the shoulders, hips, and knees.

Assistance dogs: Those canines that are specially trained to provide daily service to disabled persons, such as Seeing Eye dogs, hearing ear dogs, and those that aid people in wheelchairs.

Bait: Food or another motivating item used to focus the attention and heighten the performance of a show dog during competition.

Beagling: The traditional sport of foot hunting with a pack of Beagles.

Bites (overshot and undershot, wry, scissors, level): The *bite* is the alignment of a dog's teeth. Correct Beagle bite should be *scissors* (top incisors slightly overlapping the lower incisors) or *level* (both sets of incisors meet evenly). Incorrect bites include *overshot* (top incisors/jaw overlap and extend beyond the lower incisors with the mouth closed), *undershot* (opposite of overshot; lower jaw extends forward), and *wry* (where the jaw alignment is twisted).

Bite inhibition: Preventing a dog from ever biting down with pressure.

Bonding: Establishment of a reciprocal, trusting relationship between a dog and his owner.

Brace: A pair of hounds; also a format of field trial competition where the Beagles typically run two at a time.

Breeder: A person who breeds dogs. The AKC recognizes the owner of the female at the time of mating as the breeder of the resulting litter.

Bribe: An offer made in an attempt to coax the dog into doing something that it might prefer not to do.

Champion: A title denoting comparative quality, awarded when a dog has met specific requirements through competition at shows or trials.

Check: The point at which a hound loses the line of the rabbit while hunting.

Cherry eye: An inflamed gland of the third/inner eyelid, which protrudes to form an unsightly red lump at the inner corner of the eye.

Conformation: The structure and physical appearance of the dog in conformance with the breed standard.

Coprophagia: Consumption of feces.

Couple: Two hounds. Traditionally, hunting packs of Beagles are counted as *couples* rather than numbers of individual hounds.

Crate: A small, comfortable kennel enclosure used as a sleeping quarters and travel carrier for dogs.

Crate training: The process of teaching a dog to accept confinement to his crate; may also refer to use of the crate to teach bladder and bowl control during housebreaking.

Derby: A young hound, typically within the one-to-two-year-old range.

Draft: Denotes hounds passed from one pack to another.

Dual-purpose: Describes Beagles that possess both correct physical conformation and hunting ability.

Extinction burst: Something that can occur when you attempt to extinguish an inappropriate behavior; simply put, before your Beagle's behavior improves, it will probably get worse. When the reward for the inappropriate behavior is initially withdrawn, the hound may try even harder to get your attention.

Field trial: Competition at which the hunting ability of the dog is evaluated.

Fixture card: A listing of the hunting schedule and other planned events relating to an organized pack.

Gait: The pattern of footfall at varying rates of speed. When a handler moves his dog at a trot in the show ring, he is said to be *gaiting*.

Gundog: Any dog trained to assist his master in bringing live game to the gun, and/or retrieving the same.

Handler: The person who handles a dog at a show, field trial, or other event.

Hereditary: Genetically transmitted traits.

Hound colors: All recognized colors occurring in Beagles, Basset Hounds, Harriers, and Foxhounds. These include all shades and combinations of white (or cream), black, tan/lemon/red, brown/liver, blue/gray, and the colors of the hare or badger.

Hound glove: Grooming tool that fits over the hand like a glove. The palm area is covered with fine bristles, usually of sisal or horsehair.

Huntsman: The person who carries the horn and controls the hunting of a pack of hounds.

Instinct: An inborn, precise form of behavior. There is no knowledge behind instinct; instinctual behaviors originate from within and are hereditary, not learned.

Intelligence: The ability to think and to solve problems.

Kennel cough: Refers to any of a number of respiratory infections common to dogs.

Leg: A qualifying score toward earning an obedience title.

Level: Term indicating that the individual members of the pack should be as closely matched as possible regarding size, color and markings, speed, and running style.

Line breeding: The selective mating of dogs of the same breed that are related within a five-generation pedigree. This is done to intensify the quality genes within a bloodline.

Manners training: Instruction in housebreaking, walking politely on leash, and appropriate behavior both in the home and in public.

Master: The owner or other person responsible for overseeing the welfare of an organized pack of hounds.

Match show: An informal conformation show held primarily for practice. No championship points are awarded.

Milk teeth: The first set of smaller, puppy teeth.

National Beagle Club of America: The *parent club* (as recognized by the AKC) under which all organized foot packs are registered in the United States. The NBC is also responsible for composing the breed standard and maintains the stud books for the organized foot packs of Beagles and Basset Hounds in this country.

Neuter: To surgically remove certain reproductive organs, typically done in order to prevent accidental breedings and to contribute to the health and well-being of the dog.

Nose hug: The action of gently but firmly cupping your hand around your hound's muzzle; used to demonstrate dominance and control.

Obedience training: Training that involves teaching a dog to perform specific tasks on command.

Off game: Descibes any animals that are considered undesirable quarry for a hunting hound.

Open: To proclaim progress on a scent trail by use of voice. The dog is said to have *opened* when he begins to bark while trailing.

Pack: A group of hounds consisting of four or more members (two or more *couples*).

Pack leader: The dominant individual.

Pedigree: A written record of a dog's ancestry, typically consisting of three generations or more.

Positive reinforcement: Praise or reward typically issued for performing a desirable behavior.

Puppy: Any dog under 12 months of age.

Puppy kindergarten: An informal training class for puppies three months of age and up that provides very basic manners training and socialization.

Puppy mill: An establishment or individual that produces puppies strictly as a product for sale or resale to the general public. Potential profits take priority over the welfare or quality of the animals.

Purebred: Describes a dog whose parents both belong to the same recognized breed; usually also implies that the hounds are registered with the AKC or a similar organization.

Quarry: The game animal being pursued by a hunting hound.

Registration (full vs. limited): The recording of the breeding particulars of a dog by a purebred registry such as the AKC. *Full registration* allows for the dog to be exhibited in competitive events and to potentially be used for breeding. *Limited registration* restricts entry in conformation and Beagle field trial events, and any litters produced by the dog are ineligible for registration.

Reputable breeder: An ethical person who produces purebred puppies with the welfare of the breed at heart. Knowledgeable breeders are selective in order to produce the best possible representatives in terms of health, temperament, and breed characteristics. Quality takes preference to quantity or profit.

Rewards: A positive motivator presented *after* the appropriate behavior, as a means of reinforcement. *Primary rewards* are inherently rewarding to your Beagle, and will likely include food items, petting, and a favorite toy or activity. A *secondary reward* is something the dog has learned to accept as a reward and acknowledgment of proper behavior, such as vocal praise, a click, etc.

Separation anxiety: Distress and anxiety on the part of the dog about being separated from his pack members, characteristically resulting in disruptive, inappropriate behavior whenever he is left alone.

Socialization: The process through which a puppy develops interactive skills with other canines and humans, and learns how to respond confidently to different situations and environmental influences.

Spay: To surgically remove the female's reproductive organs to prevent conception.

Stack: To stand with feet set in perfect alignment. Dogs can *free stack* (assume this position without assistance), or may be *hard stacked* (placed into proper position by their handler).

Standard: A written description of the ideal specimen of a breed; used as a "word picture" to which dogs are compared during judging at a conformation show.

Starting: The initial portion of a dog's field training, beginning with his first venture afield and progressing to the point where he is able to follow a scent trail with a reasonable amount of control, proclaiming his progress by voice.

Starting pen: An enclosure that contains one or more tame rabbits; used to introduce a young Beagle to field work.

"Tally ho!": Call commonly used to indicate that the quarry has been viewed.

Therapy dogs: Dogs that are registered with Therapy Dogs International (or another similar organization) and provide primarily emotional service. On occasion, therapy dogs may also participate as assistants in simple forms of physical therapy at hospitals, nursing homes, or rehab centers.

Tracking: Following the scent trail left behind by a human or other animal that passed along a specific route.

Track scent: Ground scent consisting of both crushed vegetation and other odors left behind by the quarry (when hunting) or tracklayer (when tracking).

Tractability: Simply put, the professional dog trainer's fancy word for trainability. The dog's ability to learn and willingness to accept direction from his handler.

Tricolor: Markings in three colors, most typically black, white, and tan.

Vocal cordectomy (debarking): A surgical procedure to remove all or part of the vocal cords. It may not stop the Beagle from barking entirely, but does significantly reduce the volume of sound.

Whipper-in: The huntsman's assistant, who helps to maintain control of an organized foot pack.

Winners: The award given at dog shows to the one best male and one best female competing in the regular classes for their breed/variety. This is the placement that carries with it championship points.

Index